Dr. Nokkentved:

Do you remember how we thought I'd lost your book last year? I hope this makes up for it a little and that you'll find it as interesting as I found our class discussions. Thanks for everything you've taught me.

Christina S. Yee
May 12, 1995

NO TRUMPETS,
NO DRUMS

NO TRUMPETS, NO DRUMS

*A Two-State Settlement of the
Israeli-Palestinian Conflict*

MARK A. HELLER

SARI NUSSEIBEH

HILL and WANG

New York

A division of Farrar, Straus & Giroux

PUBLISHED SIMULTANEOUSLY IN CANADA BY HARPERCOLLINS*CanadaLtd*
Printed in the United States of America
DESIGNED BY TERE LOPRETE
First edition, 1991
Second printing, 1992
Library of Congress Cataloging-in-Publication Data
Heller, Mark.
No trumpets, no drums : a two-state settlement of the Israeli–
Palestinian conflict / Mark A. Heller and Sari Nusseibeh. —
1st ed.
p.   cm.
Includes index.
1. Jewish-Arab relations—1973–   2. Israel—Politics and
government.   3. Palestine—Politics and government—1948–
I. Nusseibeh, Sari.   II. Title.
DS119.7.H3854   1991   956.9405'4—dc20   91-14671   CIP

Acknowledgments

We are pleased to acknowledge the initiative and assistance of Merle Thorpe, Jr., president of the Foundation for Middle East Peace, Washington, D.C., who proposed this project, and of Gail Pressberg, former executive director of the Foundation. The Foundation was instrumental in bringing us together and providing ongoing help for our endeavor.

In writing the book, as in many other things, we were sustained by the intellectual and moral support of our wives, Barbi and Lucy. To them, and to our children, this book is dedicated.

Contents

NO TRUMPETS,
NO DRUMS

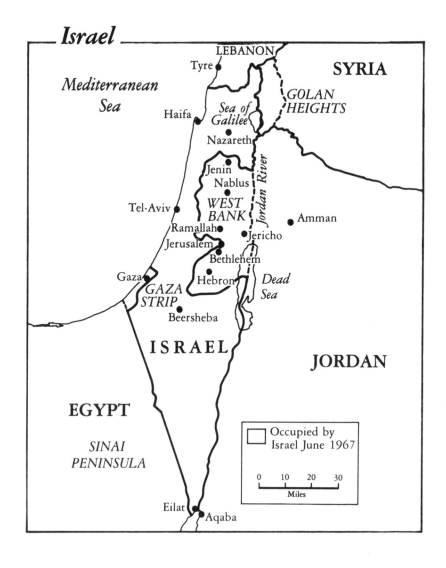

Israel

LEBANON

Tyre

SYRIA

Mediterranean
Sea

*GOLAN
HEIGHTS*

Haifa

*Sea of
Galilee*

Nazareth

Jenin

Jordan River

Nablus

Tel-Aviv

*WEST
BANK*

Amman

Ramallah

Jericho

Jerusalem

Bethlehem

Gaza

Hebron

*Dead
Sea*

*GAZA
STRIP*

Beersheba

ISRAEL

JORDAN

EGYPT

SINAI
PENINSULA

☐ Occupied by
Israel June 1967

0   10   20   30
Miles

Eilat

Aqaba

Personal Statement

MARK A. HELLER

It is never a good time for Israelis and Palestinians to meet and talk about what should be done. The burden of the past always hangs over the present and the pain of the present too often prevents any sober consideration of the future. Israelis and Palestinians are entangled with each other and alienated from one another in almost every imaginable way. In fact, their contemporary history is virtually defined by their conflict with the other. National and religious calendars commemorate ancient and modern attachments to the land over which they struggle and the course of the struggle itself: battles won or lost, disasters suffered or barely averted, pain endured or inflicted. Even if the register were closed now, it is already impossible to avoid the emotional impact of the past for very long; it is rare that a month goes by without some date of historical significance that inflames emotions. Perhaps if time stood still, it would heal all. But ongoing conflict means that the file keeps growing. The latest injury to one side becomes the cause or pretext for the next injury to the other side, and that, in turn, is duly inscribed in the collective memory, rekindling subdued passions, provoking new reactions, filling up still empty spaces in the calendar and making it harder and harder for anyone on either side to find some present time when thoughts about the possibility of future conciliation are not poisoned by the emotional scars of long ago and yesterday. No unilateral measure, whatever its technical ingenuity or tactical brilliance, can break this vicious circle of violence, retaliation, and hatred. It can only be ended by a political settlement, and promoting the search for a settlement is the reason for this book.

Although I have long held this view, being a partner in this enterprise was nevertheless a revealing experience for me. Any collaborative work is both challenging and aggravating, but in this case, the interaction with a co-author, problematic in the best of circumstances, was complicated by the fact that we wrote from opposite sides of this intense, terrible, and seemingly intractable conflict. This did not prevent the development of a good working relationship and then an unexpected but valued friendship with Sari Nusseibeh. Nevertheless, despite the fact that we were both educated in the rational academic tradition of the West, I was often startled by the differences in our basic premises, our moral calculus, and our understanding of the meaning and often even the facts of history. Perhaps those gaps can never be truly bridged, even with people such as Sari, whom I quickly came to like and respect. In any event, it soon seemed clear to me that the only broad area of agreement we could expect in this project was a programmatic one, meaning a plan of action drawn from the logic of interests and necessity rather than of rights and desires.

That kind of logic long ago drove me to a conclusion—the necessity for a two-state settlement of the Israeli-Palestinian conflict—which still seems valid from an analytical point of view but is nevertheless painful whenever I am forced to think about it. The pain is partly emotional, stemming from the need to compromise over land which has strong sentimental value. My attachment to this land was nurtured by the biblical and historical stories with which almost every Jewish child grows up, and like most Jews, I am convinced that Israel's claim to this land, including the West Bank and Gaza, is essentially just and right. I recognize that this claim cannot be exclusive, because Palestinians have lived and worked in it for a long time. I have never sought or supported the dispossession of Palestinians as individuals, and when it happens, I am saddened and embarrassed. But any inclination I might have to share the land along national lines is tempered by at least three factors:

1. My belief that any collective Palestinian claim is based on possession stemming from conquest of what was stolen property;

2. The knowledge that the Palestinians themselves view Zionism as nothing but an illegitimate modern-day counterpart of the Crusaders and that they consistently and violently opposed the idea of sharing for almost one hundred years, abandoned their absolutism only when its self-destructive effects became intolerable, and would almost certainly show no generosity if the situa-

tion were reversed and they were in control of all the land; and

3. The fact that the West Bank and Gaza, which were ruled by Arab governments before 1967, came under Israeli control as a result of a legitimate war of self-defense against unprovoked aggression.

If the rightness of Israel's claim is not absolute, it is at least better than that of its contestants, and far better than the analogous claim to some of their possessions by many outside parties who regularly castigate Israel's "intransigence" while defending without compromise their own territorial integrity. Those who demand that Israel concede the Palestinian right of self-determination while regularly resisting attempts by their own minorities to assert a similar right and studiously ignoring the brutal suppression of national and ethnic minorities elsewhere, especially in the Arab world, are guilty of hypocrisy and cynicism which rob their advocacy of any moral force.

This does not mean that the problem lacks any ethical dimension. I believe that Israel is required by its own standards to treat the Palestinians under its control with the decency and respect for elementary human rights which are due all people. While Israel's record has been far from perfect in this regard, it does compare favorably with that of other governments and armies in similar situations. Nevertheless, the suppression of Palestinian resistance compromises these standards and the mere inequality of power dulls Israeli sensibilities. For that reason, it is difficult to maintain the norms of behavior that are desirable for their own sake, regardless of any instrumental considerations, and the ethical dimension should therefore be given some weight in the debate about the future of the West Bank and Gaza. For what it's worth, my own readiness to make territorial concessions in order to permit the creation of a Palestinian state stems not from a sense of moral obligation—from the conviction that it is the right thing to do—but rather from an assessment of the constellation of local, regional, and international circumstances—that is, from an understanding that it is the wise or prudent thing to do. This does not lessen my wish that the circumstances were otherwise and that I could have peace on different terms, but wishing does not make it so, and in the larger scheme of things, it doesn't matter that much whether Israel draws this conclusion reluctantly or embraces it enthusiastically. The important thing is that Israel voluntarily reach what I believe to be the correct understanding, because it is grounded in a reality that will almost certainly not change to Israel's advantage in the future.

Israelis and Palestinians are destined to live with each other, one way or another. The choice is between the ways: continued stalemate or a two-state settlement. This is sometimes defined as a choice between territory and peace, although that oversimplifies the situation. On the one hand, Israel can retain possession of the territory and there will surely be no peace. There may also be no war, though this cannot be said with much confidence; Arab motivation to change the status quo will be intense and the region will, like the Balkans before World War I, remain a powder keg that can be detonated by any number of sparks. But even if a major explosion is avoided, the state of war will exact a continuing toll of death, injuries, and disrupted lives, expose Israel to constant pressures, distort its priorities, and limit the resources available to house, educate, and employ its existing population and the hundreds of thousands of immigrants expected in the coming years. The alternative is for Israel to give up much of the West Bank and Gaza and permit the Palestinians to run their own lives in a state of their own, recognizing in practice what the Palestinians (and much of the rest of the world) consider to be their elementary right to independence and self-determination. Israelis do not have to share the Palestinian belief that this right is axiomatic and unconditional. They do not have to admit that they have been the bad guys and the Palestinians the good guys, or even that both sides have been both bad and good in equal degree. But they do have to understand that satisfying this Palestinian aspiration, at least to the extent that it does not pose an unacceptable danger, provides the only chance for a stable peace.

Israel's concession is not absolute, since it will still have a military presence in the areas and Israelis will still be able to work, trade, travel, or even live there (perhaps even more safely than now), but neither is the reward: the peace may not be stable or lasting or absolute. On balance, however, I believe that this formula is the basis of a properly constructed political settlement which will make Israel stronger, more secure, and more prosperous than it would be in a situation of permanent stalemate. Such a settlement, including appropriate security arrangements, will hardly affect Israel's deterrent power but will markedly reduce the Palestinian and Arab motivation to fight and may very well open up a wide range of new political and economic opportunities—at home, throughout the Middle East, and around the world.

The criteria for judging whether or not a settlement is properly constructed cannot be precise. However, a package of elements that seems necessary to maximize stability and minimize risks has emerged from widespread debate, the lessons of history, and common sense, and this package forms the core of the settlement proposed in this book. Its leading elements are:

1. A full-fledged peace agreement with the Palestinians, meaning explicit Palestinian renunciation of all subsequent territorial and other claims against Israel, including the right of Palestinian refugees to move to Israel without Israeli permission;

2. Provision for resolution of the Palestinian refugee problem through resettlement outside of Israel and material compensation, coupled with compensation for material losses of Jews from Arab countries;

3. Transitional arrangements, including phased implementation of the agreement, in order to build confidence and test compliance;

4. Security arrangements, including limitations on Palestinian military capabilities, maintaining in place most of Israel's military infrastructure in the territories during a specified transition period, and creating significant early-warning, intelligence-gathering, and combat capabilities for an unspecified period of time thereafter;

5. Preserving access to essential water resources;

6. Preserving the physical unity of Jerusalem and its status as Israel's capital;

7. Ensuring that the two-state settlement is an integral part of a comprehensive Israeli-Arab settlement, based on political agreements with the major Arab states, regional security arrangements to reduce the overall military threat, and establishment of normal relations with potentially great economic benefits.

If Israel can secure this sort of settlement, it will not have the territories, but it may gain peace, or at least a sounder relationship with itself, the region, and the rest of the world. Even if peace, security, and prosperity were assured, it would not be easy to choose this course because the price—part of the national homeland—is high. But as a value judgment that each person must make according to his own scales of what is most important, I have long been convinced that the price is worthwhile.

Of course, peace, security, and prosperity are not assured, and choosing between the stalemate and a two-state settlement therefore depends on weighing risks as well as costs and benefits. I know of no method for judging precisely the likelihood of future political events. The only mathematical measure of probability that has any significance is 50 percent; when we have no basis for guessing whether or not something will happen, we say (like all gamblers) that the chances are 50-50. Otherwise, the most we can do is to assign qualitative estimates of probabilities to various risks, and whatever terms we use are likely to convey an exaggerated sense of precision. With these limitations in mind, I have tried to evaluate the basic risks involved in the kind of settlement outlined here. My calculus is as follows:

1. I hope that a peace settlement will lead to the complete normalization of Israel's role as a political, cultural, commercial, and touristic actor in the Middle East and to the development of a full range of harmonious state relations and personal ties between it and its Arab neighbors. I will be disappointed if this does not happen, but not really surprised. This may happen

over time, but it is just as likely that some nonsecurity dimension of the peace agreements envisaged here will not be upheld, resulting in a political and/or economic shortfall in the "peace dividend."

2. Even if "full peace" on the model of Western Europe is not achieved or maintained, it is highly unlikely that Palestinian or other Arab violations of the agreements will endanger Israeli security interests to the point where a large-scale military response is necessary. In their heart of hearts, Palestinians and other Arabs may never fully reconcile themselves to the legitimacy of Israel's existence, but the urgency of their opposition and the blood and treasure they are prepared to spend in order to fight it will decline dramatically in the aftermath of a settlement which gives the Palestinians something important to safeguard. In other words, there is very little chance that the likelihood of a major war will rise because of these peace agreements. In case a war does take place, however, I believe that Israel will be strong enough to win decisively with conventional means, and after having made the sacrifices and taken the risks of a peace settlement and nevertheless been forced to fight again, it would be fully justified in reoccupying the territories and permanently changing their political status. Nevertheless, even a victorious war would be a tragedy, because lives would have been lost.

3. There is, of course, a very slight danger that Israel could not cope with a military threat through conventional means. In the language of probability theory, the compound risk that this would happen is minute, but it is still a possibility, and one that is still too serious to be blithely dismissed. If it did happen, Israel would be obliged to rely on unconventional weapons and/or outside intervention. This would be a disaster.

4. Even worse is the nightmarish prospect that nothing would avail. This risk is virtually, though not absolutely, nonexistent, but it should be remembered that the compound risk of ultimate catastrophe—that is, that unconventional weapons and/or outside intervention would fail to work after conventional defense had failed—is at least as great if war results from the absence of a peace settlement, and perhaps greater. In the morbid calculus of this analysis, the risk that a comprehensive peace settlement based on two states will lead to the ultimate catastrophe for Israel is infinitesimal.

Assuming that these estimates bear some relationship to reality, two questions must be answered. The first is: "Do the possible benefits justify the risks?" The benefits of a "real peace" with the Arab world would be immense, but there is no more than an even chance that real peace will prevail long into the future. Even limited or strained relations—a cold peace—with the Arab world would provide partial or intermittent advantages which might justify the limited, considered risks of a two-state settlement as outlined here; the relevant model here is the peace agreement with Egypt, which has not produced an idyllic relationship but is nevertheless seen, with good reason, as a significant gain for Israel. If the only question were one of risks and benefits, there would still be a case for taking a chance but it would not be overwhelming, because the consequences of being wrong are so great that risks of this sort should probably be avoided, whatever the possible benefits.

This obviously raises a second question: "Why take any risk at all?" The simple answer is that if a no-risk alternative existed, I would prefer it. Unfortunately, there is no risk-free policy. The alternative to a two-state settlement which involves some risks but holds out a chance for peace is a policy of stalemate, which also involves risks but holds out no chance of peace. Comparing the risks of the two alternatives is complicated, because the same factors may operate in different directions. For example, the status quo makes the Arab motivation to fight much greater, making war more likely, but control of the territories also improves Israel's tactical position (though by how much, as compared to the security arrangements outlined in this book, is not self-evident), and this may contribute to deterrence of Arab attackers, making war somewhat less likely. In this sense, it may be argued that retention of the territories both harms and helps Israel's strategic position.

However, Israel pays a price for its containment of Palestinian resistance, meaning that it runs political, economic, and social risks every day. These, too, have strategic implications. The occupation, though no longer as cheap as it was before the start of the intifada, is still tolerable. But it does result in a constant stream of Israeli casualties, military and civilian, and it forces Israel to invest resources in riot control and police operations that could be more productively applied to civilian purposes or the buildup and modernization of the Israel Defense Forces. Domestically, the occupation also contributes to the growing radicalization of Israeli Arabs and threatens the tolerance for dissent, even among Jews, without which a democratic political culture cannot survive. At the international level, the conflict with the Palestinians means continued conflict with the Arab world. The two may not be logically connected, but the political linkage between them is strong. Attitudes toward *the Palestinians* are not uniformly positive in the Arab world, and much of whatever goodwill they previously enjoyed was dissipated by their behavior during the Gulf crisis. But devotion to *the cause of Palestine* has always been strong and will remain so in most Arab countries. Even President Sadat, who was the object of so much criticism for having allegedly made a separate peace with Israel, insisted that the peace treaty explicitly incorporate a framework for settling the Palestinian question. More recently, Saddam Hussein's cynicism in championing the Palestinian cause was too transparent to keep other Arab states out of the coalition against him, but it did put them on the defensive. Concern about the impact of Israeli involvement on Arab resolve to confront Saddam was a constant factor throughout the crisis: American efforts to forge and maintain the coalition conspicuously excluded Israel; Israel was obliged to maintain a "low profile"; the Bush Administration uncharacteristically supported a Security Council resolution condemning Israel after the killings on the Temple Mount in October 1990; American leaders who came to consult with regional partners before and during the fighting consistently bypassed Israel; and Israeli self-restraint following the Scud missile attacks (whatever the other considerations may have been) was explained as responsiveness to American concern about the effect on the coalition of a visible Israeli role in the war. In short, the Gulf crisis was further evidence of the symbiotic relationship between Israeli-Palestinian and Israeli-Arab conflicts. We might wish it to be otherwise, but the relationship is undeniable and it is difficult to imagine any resolution of the latter without some minimally acceptable resolution of the former. If these two conflicts are not resolved, Israel will have to go on devoting a huge share of its national resources—its talent, time, and money—to these problems, with the corresponding risk that too little will be left for the things—education, health care, housing, modern industrial plant, technological innovation, transportation and communications infrastructure—that are needed to make Israel a more attractive place in which to live and to enable it to compete economically in the next century. These are not just hypothetical risks: the successful absorption of the hundreds of thousands of Jewish immigrants from the Soviet Union and perhaps even their continued willingness to come or stay in Israel are jeopardized by the chronic housing shortage and the specter of widespread unemployment. The aliyah of Soviet Jews to Israel is an opportunity of historic dimensions, both for Soviet Jews and for Israel, and if it is squandered, that will be a tragedy (or a crime) of equal proportions.

If a cost of ongoing conflict is the distorted use of Israel's scarce resources, the risk is that its resources will become still scarcer in the future. Iraqi missile attacks produced a brief surge of sympathy for Israel, but this was a deviation from a long-term trend. It has been many years since Israel has been perceived as an embattled underdog with no choice but to fight against implacable and uncompromising enemies. Even its most ardent sympathizers and supporters abroad (including diaspora Jewry) no longer accept that Arab intransigence and Israeli vulnerability justify any and all policies. Instead, Israeli actions and positions are judged by some vague but nevertheless limiting standard of "reasonableness." If Israel is increasingly found wanting in this respect and held responsible for the stalemate, there is a serious danger that the moral and material assistance it receives will diminish. And that will affect Israel's ability to deter or fight a war and to resist an imposed settlement, probably on worse terms than those outlined here.

In the last analysis, everyone must make his or her own judgment about the costs and risks of a stalemate and decide whether or not a two-state settlement is worthwhile. Obviously, my own position is that this is the least undesirable choice from a short and not very appealing list of options. But while I am confident in my conclusion, I cannot be absolutely certain. Since the issue is one of analysis and not of religious faith, I have constantly tried to reexamine my position in the light of new developments or new arguments, while keeping my own passions under control.

This is not an easy thing to do. There is an emotional climate that encourages Israelis and Jews to stick a "pro-Palestinian" label on this position and to deny the possibility that it may actually be "pro-Israeli" in the sense that it best serves the interests of the country they love. People who view compromise as a natural and legitimate feature of their private and business lives, of their relations with relatives, friends, neighbors, and co-workers, and of the normal flow of domestic and international politics, often switch to a different mind-set when the issue of the territories and Israeli-Palestinian relations arises and proceed as if compromise here is equivalent to political and religious heresy. Too many self-appointed guardians of Jewish virtue wrap themselves in a mantle of patriotism and vilify, not just the positions of their opponents, but also their personal motives and integrity. In the best of circumstances, it is difficult for "bleeding hearts" and "PLO-niks" to argue the advantages of a settlement based on compromise with the Palestinians.

But though I resent the populists and demagogues

who turn political debates into loyalty tests, I resent even more the Palestinians who help these people prosper. Every new Palestinian outrage fortifies Israeli hard-liners in the moral high ground they have claimed for themselves, and such outrages are depressingly frequent. During the time that this book was being written, Palestinians murdered dozens of Israeli civilians going about their ordinary, everyday business—not rioting, not demonstrating, not attacking, not provoking—in the buses, fields, streets, and markets of Israel, and the list would have been much longer if a coastal attack by the Abul Abbas faction of the Palestine Liberation Front (part of the PLO which had previously "renounced" terrorism) had not been foiled. And Palestinian preachers, after spreading false rumors of a Jewish plot to build the Third Temple on the Feast of Tabernacles, incited thousands of Palestinians to gather on the Temple Mount, where they attacked police forces and Jews praying at the Western Wall. Even more damaging was the Palestinians' endorsement of Saddam's belligerent anti-Israel rhetoric in early 1990, their support for his invasion of Kuwait in August, and then their identification with him during the war against the American-led coalition. The most outrageous thing of all was the sight of the Palestinians in the West Bank and Gaza cheering from their rooftops as Iraqi Scud missiles fell on Israel and calling on Saddam to use chemical weapons, even as they demanded free gas masks from the Israeli government.

Palestinian actions reflect the impulses, hysteria, and frustration of individuals or the political failures of organizational leaders unwilling to challenge mass sentiment. Murderers of Israeli citizens, for example, are normally inspired by personal revenge, religious fanaticism, or the need to defend against imagined Jewish threats or provocations. Indeed, what most Palestinian actions have in common is that their explanation is emotional, not political. They are not calculated to promote the objective of a peace settlement or otherwise serve the "Palestinian cause" (although the Temple Mount riot, which resulted in the killing of seventeen Palestinians, did lead to widespread international condemnation of Israel), but they nevertheless do have an important political effect: the further hardening of public opinion in Israel.

Each incident involving the death or injury of civilians undermines the sense of personal security among Israelis. But it also strengthens the belief that the Palestinians are addicted to mindless, indiscriminate violence and that their hostility is permanent and irreconcilable. It reaffirms the determination of those Israelis who oppose any compromise with the Palestinians and seems to oblige advocates of a peaceful settlement—as if they are somehow the spokesmen of the Palestinians—to explain the unexplainable and defend the indefensible, thus further undermining the force of their arguments.

Palestinian support for Saddam Hussein has had a particularly devastating effect. Israelis on the right were exhilarated because all their prognoses seemed to have been borne out. Yasir Arafat's embrace of Saddam looked like "reversion to type," an instinctive abandonment of principles only grudgingly and insincerely accepted shortly before, and a more faithful reflection of Palestinian attitudes toward peaceful coexistence and the sanctity of any future Israeli-Palestinian border. Rightists took comfort in the belief that the Gulf crisis, by finally exposing the "truth" about the marginal importance of the Palestinian problem for Middle Eastern stability and about the "real" character of the Palestinians and of Arab politics, would distract world attention, discredit the PLO, and eliminate, or at least defer to the indefinite future, the need to resolve the Israeli-Palestinian conflict. And among Israelis who could be termed the "sentimental left"—those who tend to draw their political understanding primarily from personal encounters with "nice" Palestinians, simple images of right and wrong, and anger at the obtuseness of their own governments—there was widespread disillusionment and despair. Many of these people had much invested in the image of Palestinians as innocent victims of a conflict prolonged solely by Israeli inflexibility, as the embodiment of right, truth, justice, goodness, generosity, moderation, and altruism, and they reacted to Palestinian identification with Saddam Hussein as though Mother Teresa had been caught skimming off contributions to pay for pornographic videotapes. Shocked by this demonstration of vicious hostility and of the Palestinians' ability to interpret selectively the universal principles on which they base their claims against Israel, many on the left seemed to forget the dictum that peace has to be made with enemies, and they abandoned hope for a peaceful settlement with such unfriendly people.

There is no justification for either the agonized reappraisal of the left or the self-congratulation of the right. Palestinian behavior with respect to Iraq, both before and during the Gulf crisis, was undoubtedly self-destructive. Indeed, Palestinian leaders have often preferred to act on instinct or to permit irrational displays of popular sentiment to prevail over collective self-interest (though they are hardly unique in this respect). All this indicates, however, is the necessity for a strong safety net against irrationality in any settlement; it does nothing to negate the need for a settlement per se. As for Palestinian ill will, it is surprising that some people were surprised. Palestinian attitudes are a product of specific circumstances—a prolonged conflict with Israel in which they have decisively lost almost every round, the failure of both a costly intifada and a major political initiative to produce tangible gains, the demonstrated inability of all leaders and all ideologies in the Arab world to advance their cause, and widespread social and economic deprivation. To assume that intense Palestinian hatred of Israel will endure forever, regardless of the circumstances—especially whether or not the conflict has been resolved by mutual agreement—is to assume that it is part of some genetic code. There is no basis for such an assumption. Suspicion and distrust may well persist between Israelis and Palestinians, as they do among many other nationalities with a history of contradictions, but attitudes and conflicts feed on each other, and the extent and intensity of Palestinian hatred will almost certainly decline in the aftermath of a settlement. The Israeli left, however, was disappointed because they seemed to expect that goodwill would emerge even before a settlement. This is touching, but naïve. Goodwill cannot emerge without tangible movement toward a settlement, but a settlement does not depend on goodwill; all that it requires is a proper understanding by each side of its own real interests.

Even more naïve is the belief of the right that Saddam Hussein's aggression and Yasir Arafat's support for it have made Israel's Palestinian problem disappear. Iraq's actions may have heightened international sensitivity to Israel's security concerns, but they did nothing to broaden support for Israel's territorial claims or reduce concern about the Palestinians and the threat that the unresolved conflict poses to Middle Eastern stability. On the contrary, the linkage of the Gulf crisis to Israeli control of the West Bank and Gaza advocated so forcefully by Saddam, most Palestinians, and many other Arabs appears to have been accepted, in practice. The only substantive parallel between these two situations is that they both resulted from Arab aggression—Egyptian, Jordanian, and Syrian in 1967, Iraqi in 1990. And until Iraq was expelled from Kuwait in early 1991, Western leaders generally rejected demands to connect them. But as soon as the war against Iraq ended, the same Western leaders turned with renewed vigor to the Palestinian problem, as though the one followed automatically from the other.

It is difficult to predict how the United States will pursue the quest for a settlement and, therefore, what the long-term effect will be on U.S.-Israeli relations. Disillusioned by Palestinian behavior during the Gulf crisis, the United States may try to extract a quid pro quo from those Arab states that sought and received its protection against Iraq. Alternatively, American leaders may simply revert to pre-1990 "business as usual," which was not always satisfactory from Israel's point of view, or even tire of the whole problem. However, they may also conclude that consolidating ties with newfound Arab allies and institutionalizing security arrangements in the Gulf require them to "reward" those allies by dealing actively with the Israeli-Arab conflict—that is, by exerting heavy pressure on Israel to be more "flexible" on the Palestinian question.

And even if this danger is averted, there is a more fundamental factor that will not change—the Palestinians themselves. The current Palestinian leadership, organizational structure, and political basis have been discredited among many Arab states and perhaps even among some Palestinians because of the PLO's close identification with Saddam Hussein. For most Israelis, the PLO has always been irretrievably tainted. But as the conceptual incarnation of a collective Palestinian identity, it is probably indestructible. And whatever transformations it undergoes, the Palestinians will not go away.

I do not share the view that Palestinians, as individuals, will necessarily be freer, more prosperous, or more fulfilled in an independent state; contrary to the sanguine prognosis in my co-author's addendum, I consider it entirely possible that after the euphoria of independence passes, a Palestinian state will join the depressingly long list of economically and spiritually stagnant dictatorships in the Third World. But as long as the Palestinians are kept under Israeli rule against their will and denied the chance to try ruling themselves, Israel will be the reason for their discontent and the focus of their hostility. Sometimes they will express their resistance in sullen, passive ways, sometimes through low-level subversion and sporadic attacks, sometimes through large-scale violent demonstrations. If there were no reasonable alternative, Israel would be justified in opposing this resistance. And whatever the alternatives, it can probably sustain this course for a long time to come. But a better alternative may exist—in the settlement outlined in this book—and if Israel nevertheless chooses to maintain the present course and refrains from exploring the other one, it will do itself grievous injury by spurning the chance for a better future that its people want, need, and deserve.

My greatest hope, of course, is that this book will in

some way help to promote the Israeli-Palestinian agreement on which that better future depends. However, I have no illusions about the power of the written word to change history, and if the only result is that a few people begin to think a little differently, that, too, will be a source of satisfaction. But whatever the impact may be, the book has at least given me a new colleague and friend.

Personal Statement

SARI NUSSEIBEH

I did not feel comfortable when I first met last year with Mark Heller in the Washington offices of the Foundation for Middle East Peace to discuss this project. His ostensibly defiant attitude, even his initial disinclination to predicate our joint effort on the premise of a two-state solution, almost made me decide to give up on the project even as it was in its initial planning stage. Two overwhelming forces dominated my state of mind: On the one hand, there were my emotions as a Palestinian (probably expressed outwardly in the form of a defiant attitude on my part), which were a constantly ready source for rebellion and rejection at the smallest sign of slight on the part of my Israeli interlocutor. On the other hand, reason told me that, because of the background to these emotions, a way must be plowed, together with my interlocutor, whoever he or she may be, into a better future. In this interplay of forces, only one factor, only one imperative, stood to tilt the balance in my mind one way or the other: whether my Israeli interlocutor recognized the principle of equitability and mutuality between our two peoples. Mark Heller's apparent initial preference to have the work indifferently address different scenarios, and to treat the two-state scenario as just one of them, made me feel that he did not start from the premise of equitability, and therefore I was not sure that I could work closely with someone who felt this way. Moreover, my prior knowledge that he had already and independently expressed his preference for a two-state solution made me suspect that he was in a sense already trying to "play politics" or "gain advantage" in this meeting by aiming through our planned project to reduce the two-state scenario from the realm of the necessary (or what is agreed upon) to the realm of the dimly possible (or what is debatable). Either way, the emotions his attitude provoked in me brought me a hairbreadth away from deciding not to participate in this project. However, the meeting was conducted to a positive end, thanks primarily to the skillful navigation of our hosts. The decision was taken at the end of the meeting to go ahead with the project, and once begun, a positive working relationship developed between Mark Heller and me and surprisingly, in view of how it all started, also an esteemed friendship.

I give this somewhat personal account because I believe it provides an important insight into the psychological framework within which any Israeli-Palestinian negotiation, however ostensibly technical only, will be conducted. So sensitive are the issues involved, so paranoid the actors, that even the first tentative steps toward addressing them must be absolutely right. In my view, the principle of mutual recognition, the recognition by each side of the other side's right to self-determination, can guarantee not only an initial engagement in negotiations but also an inbuilt mutual confidence mechanism to support what is bound to turn out to be an arduous and lengthy process of negotiation.

This viewpoint was reinforced by many "incidents" that occurred in the course of our joint work—an effort that turned out to be perhaps less a jointly written text than a negotiated product. A salient example is the chapter on security arrangements. During our discussions on this chapter, Mark's insistence on the presence of trip-wire units, at least for a transitional period, was something I couldn't make sense of to begin with on security grounds. Therefore I suspected it simply to be a surreptitious means of prolonging the occupation. But so genuinely positive had our joint work been by then that I was at least prepared to consider his arguments. Finally, they seemed to make sense to me, and therefore I accepted them. Of course, I may still be wrong in my judgments, but the point is that rational persuasion is possible only if there is the correct predisposition—in this case, the trust that the basic assumptions are not in question but what is under debate is the formulation that will most suitably translate these assumptions into a practical reality. I have long subscribed to the view that while Palestinians will not and cannot regard the principle of their sovereignty to be open to question, it is only natural that they accept the need to negotiate over the degree to which they can exercise this sovereignty. In this, they would not be different from many other countries and nations which "willingly" learn to live with certain restrictions in their military or economic activities, not because this is the best of all possible worlds, but because this is the best possible use of this one.

This brings me to a second major observation regarding this work, and it is perhaps an observation that is mostly addressed to the Palestinian reader. On reading this text, many Palestinians will very likely feel, perhaps not quite dissatisfaction, but a definite lack of satisfaction. If I may presume to speak about the Israeli public, I believe a rather similar feeling will also prevail, although only among that group of people who are already opposed to any territorial concessions. The distinction is that among Palestinians this feeling will prevail even among those who support a two-state solution. The observation that I wish to make here is that a two-state solution cannot be worked out without Israeli agreement, and an Israeli agreement cannot be forthcoming except in the context of the existing balance of power in the region. There are those who will argue for a radical transformation of the existing balance of power before any negotiations are entered into. My response to this argument is that, before one dismisses the Palestinian state which is outlined in this work, however unsatisfactory it might seem, one should carefully and realistically make up a balance sheet that enumerates the costs that will be incurred in the process of this hypothetical transformation, as against the incremental benefits that could be achieved for a Palestinian state as a result of it. In my opinion, if one considers these overall costs and benefits, and weighs them against the benefits, both actual and potential, that will accrue from establishing the state more or less outlined in this work, one is bound to reach the conclusion that it is more rational to work with this solution rather than against it.

In this context, I feel particularly satisfied with the provision, mentioned in the chapter on implementation, which requires that an open debate take place in the

Palestinian community, to be followed by a general plebiscite which will determine whether or not the people are behind this solution. In itself, such a provision will at least facilitate a rational consideration of the option. Very often in Arab society, because of the lack of maturity of democratic institutions and practices, policies are decided on "behind people's backs," as it were, and almost in secret. This inevitably gives rise to the suspicion that such policies are not in the people's best interests, and are inspired conspiratorially by "hidden" or "foreign" evil forces. Also inevitably for this reason, new ideas are often shot down as soon as they are floated. More tragically, the individuals themselves who stand behind those ideas are sometimes also shot down, whether physically or politically. Such tendencies can at least partly be explained against the background of the absence, or near-absence, of democratic procedures in the process of decision making. This absence leaves people no choice but to suspect that something is going to be imposed on them against their will, as much as against their interest, and that force or intimidation is the only means available to abort it. If, on the other hand, it is made clear right from the outset that any and all terms which are agreed upon in negotiations will still have to be ratified by the people, so that each individual would have as much right as any other individual to participate in formulating the final decision, then at least negotiations themselves will be given a chance, and the outcome of the negotiations can be given the studied attention it deserves. The disadvantage of this provision is, of course, that an arrangement which is in the best interest of a community runs the risk of being aborted through the democratic process, or at any rate of being delayed and stretched out. But in words similar to those Churchill once used, this still remains the least evil of other forms of government and decision-making procedures.

However, to go back to the point mentioned earlier, it is indisputable that the general guidelines outlined in this work reflect an unequal balance. I would regard it, not as an inequality in the balance of principles, but rather as an inequality in the balance of power. I would regard it, more specifically, as a reflection of the degree to which a principle can be exercised within the framework of a given balance of power. There is a fundamental difference between these two types of inequalities, and my argument to the Palestinian reader would be that as long as the principle is preserved, then given the reality of the balance of power and all the calculus that can be derived from it, the inequality in question is one which can be lived with. Naturally, the situation would be different if the principle itself is challenged. In this case, I do not believe that any amount of rationalism or pragmatism would in the circumstances be realistic: there is a bottom line beyond which no self-respecting human being can go. For Palestinians, I would submit that this bottom line is the establishment of an independent Palestinian state, more or less along the Green Line, with East Jerusalem as its capital. This bottom line preserves the required equitability in principle, because it is predicated on mutuality. However, once negotiations on this basis proceed, its exact meaning will have to be defined by what is perforce an inequality in the balance of power. It is inconceivable that the compromise solution reached will not reflect this existing balance of power.

There is yet a third kind of inequality, or what one should perhaps call "asymmetry," which I have come to learn about in the course of my discussions with my colleague. If one consciously sets all rights and feelings aside, and proceeds to think purely on the basis of self-interest—which basically describes the procedure we tried to employ in writing this text—one is bound to accept that Israel's territorial withdrawal constitutes an immediate material gain for Palestinians, and only a long-term material gain for Israel. Therefore, Israel's concessions, having been accorded already, are in no need of guarantees on this score; while Palestinian concessions, being initially verbal rather than material, would still be due and are thus in need of such guarantees. In this way, Israel is compelled to institute safeguards and make demands of the Palestinians which will guarantee that Israel's long-term gain is realized. Because, while the Israeli concession is immediate, the corresponding Palestinian concession can only be derived in the course of time.

I therefore distinguish in my mind between (at least) two aspects of "restrictions" on the Palestinian state outlined in this work: one aspect relates to the inequality in the balance of power (perhaps the sharing of aquifers falls under this heading, or the type of connection or linkage between Gaza and the West Bank), while another relates to the asymmetry involved in the nature of the bargain that will be achieved in negotiations (perhaps the time factor in the implementation program and the deployment of forces would be examples reflecting this).

I would submit that these are restrictions with which Palestinians can learn to live. Admittedly, Palestinians will find all such aspects of restriction burdensome. But if these restrictions constitute a first-level irritant, the problem deeper down that many of them have traditionally had with any compromise solution relates more to their overall outlook on their predicament. While it is more important to set out an emotion-free outline of a compromise solution which is in the self-interest of both parties, it is still important to have an appreciation of the underlying domain of perceived rights and emotions from which this solution has to be retrieved. Bluntly put, Palestinians essentially believe that any bargaining with Israel over Palestinian territory is like bargaining over stolen property with the very thief who stole it by force. Essentially, the Palestinians regard themselves as the rightful indigenous inheritors of all the Arab communities that have settled in this region since time immemorial. Unlike the Jews, who were dispossessed of a territorial (and therefore objective) continuity and who perhaps therefore compensated for this through a highly developed sense of continuous collective self-consciousness, Palestinian Arab continuity has been objective rather than subjective. Thus, while it may be true that there is no subjective thread (until the emergence of Islam) linking the various Arab communities who lived and ruled in Palestine through history, yet this is not regarded by present-day Palestinians as in any sense undermining their historical rightful claim to the country, or their claim to be the rightful descendants of the Jebusites, the Canaanites, the Philistines, etc. The absence of a continuity in collective self-consciousness is not an argument against objective title and rights. Thus the very first entry of Jewish tribes into Palestine from the Iraq region is already regarded as a settlement wave into what is essentially a Palestinian Arab region.

As to the biblical promise to Jews and the corollary claim to a title deed, this is not regarded as relating to the present-day Israelis, in any case by many Palestinians, while those who see a connection between biblical Jews and present-day Israelis see this connection from the perspective of the Holy Koran: "We have judged to the Israelites in the Book that twice they shall cause corruption in the earth, and that they shall be raised very high. Once the time is due for the first promise, We shall send unto you men of great strength, who will penetrate the lands, and the promise shall be fulfilled. Then we shall give you the upper hand against them, and allow you to accumulate wealth and children, and We shall make you greater in number. If you are to do good, then it is for yourselves, but if you are to do evil, then it is against yourselves; and once it is time for the second promise, then they shall draw a veil of misery on your faces, and they shall enter the mosque as they have done the first time, and they shall raze down to the ground what has been built. May God be merciful unto you, and if you turn against Us then We shall turn against you, meting out punishment to you in Hell" (al-Isra', 4–8). Many Moslems interpret these words which God addresses to the Jews to mean that the (present) ingathering of the Jews in Palestine is inevitable, but so is the confrontation with them, and their final defeat. Others take these words to indicate an inevitable fulfillment of the part relating to the building up of the Israelite strength, leaving subsequent developments conditional on Israel's behavior. Either way, the forceful ingathering of the Israelites, which is perceived as carried out on the basis of the infliction of pain and suffering on the Palestinians, and therefore on the basis of injustice, is regarded as an omen for a major subsequent confrontation. In the final analysis, all views, religious and nonreligious, converge on the perception that Israel's establishment by force, and its continued forceful occupation of the territories won in 1967, is simply unjust. To go back therefore to the discussion on compromise solutions, Palestinians have a basic problem with accepting compromise solutions—let alone restrictions in such solutions—because they believe this would be submitting to injustice.

Besides the historical or religious perspectives with which this conflict is viewed by Palestinians, causing discomfort with the very idea of compromise solutions, and in any case undermining any religious claims by Israel in Palestinian eyes, there is also an immediate practical negative imprint by Israel on the life of practically every Palestinian family, once again making the very idea of a compromise discomforting. To make this aspect more vivid to the reader, I would like once again to go back to my first meeting with Mark Heller. As I sat across the table from Mark in the Washington offices of the Foundation for Middle East Peace, I strongly sensed an asymmetry in the balance of justice. Not in any sense meaning to show disrespect for Mark or open any wound which Mark as a Jew suffered, still I couldn't help observing that I, whose own family is rooted in Jerusalem for at least twelve hundred continuous years, was compelled to be making a deal with a Canadian immigrant. My mother's family, in the course of the setting up of the Israeli state, had been turned into refugees, with my grandmother eventually dying in exile. Her husband belonged to a first generation of Palestinians who had to undergo temporary deportation, detention in exile, and the demolition of their house at the hands of the British Mandatory authorities in Palestine. (He still managed on his return from exile to be elected mayor of Ramle for two years before he died of a heart attack in 1948.) My own father had to live his entire adult life, until his death in 1986, suffering from an amputation of one of his legs which had developed gangrene as a result of an Israeli-inflicted bullet wound in 1948. Until this day many members of my family, on my mother's side and on my father's, are prevented from returning to live in Palestine. Many of my immediate relatives or friends had more recently suffered one or another of the occupation's punitive or preventive measures. In other words, to me the question is not one of numbers or figures, nor is it a question of pontification and historical or political theory: it is a cause of immediate hardship and pain, of fear and anticipation. And the case of my family and circle of acquaintances and friends is not special; if anything, my family has suffered far less cumulative pain and hardship than the average Palestinian family, which has typically suffered deaths and deprivation, hunger and destitution. All of it, of course, in the context of Israel's establishment and the prolongation of occupation.

I make mention of all of this, not by way of scoring points or writing history, but in order to reveal the full array of Palestinian emotions embedded in the perception of Israel. Besides the absence of democracy, which prompts them to suspect and oppose outright the idea of a compromise solution, Palestinians are thus already imbued with a sense of their own righteousness that is at odds with that very idea. These elements combine to explain the historical Palestinian rejection of Israel and of compromises with it. Historically, very few people could look beyond this sense of injustice—indeed, could exercise reason beyond pain—to see the value of compromise. My aforementioned grandfather, who was also a member of the Arab Higher Committee which formed the Palestinian leadership in the 1940s, belonged to a minority which subscribed to the view of accepting the 1947 Partition Plan. However, both he in the mainstream leadership and what was then called the "Palestinian Opposition" formed only a minority. Nonetheless, the seed of compromise was already there, and I have it from my own father that during his own period of recuperation after the amputation of his leg, he had received the authorization from the Mufti himself (Haj Amin al-Husseini) to investigate the possibility of using Britain's offices to mediate with Israel over the implementation of the Partition Plan. However, so sensitive was the issue that as soon as one British reporter leaked the news to the press (it is still a mystery how he got wind of the affair), my father promptly packed up and returned from London to Cairo, having aborted the mission, and handed back to the Mufti his written authorization.

In an address to the Radical Society meeting in London in 1989, Hani al-Hasan, a co-founder of Fatah and a member of its Central Committee, traces the origins of the PLO leadership's tentative steps toward a compromise solution with Israel to the late 1960s. However, even if such tendencies existed at the level of sectors within the leadership, there was obviously little or no public support for them. Even so, the voices for a compromise solution within the Palestinian national movement grew during the 1970s and found expression in various events and figures. Among such events were the proceedings of the Palestine National Council (PNC) during its 1973 session, where the idea of "establishing a national authority on any part of Palestine to be liberated" was formally adopted. The Stages Plan, as it was dubbed, has come under heavy attack from Israeli propagandists and politicians for belying the true intention of Palestinians to pursue their strategy of the "annihilation of Israel." Beyond propaganda, this session constituted a conceptual leap, to my mind, in the direction of accepting a two-state solution. For the first time in the national strategy of Palestinians, a major shift in political vision was achieved, where the issue of national identity came to supersede that of territory as a number-one priority item. Already, a break was being made, however tentative, from the emotion-laden past. Furthermore, one could understand how and why the call for a state in the West Bank/Gaza could not have been made before that time, and in particular during the years from 1949 to 1967. The Palestinian national psychology was undergoing a radical transformation in the way the issues of territory and identity were being perceived. During the following year one of Palestine's top-ranking political thinkers, Walid al-Khalidi, published his controversial paper "Thinking the Unthinkable" in *Foreign Affairs* in the United States, where he set out the outlines of a (demilitarized) Palestinian state living at peace alongside Israel. Intellectual debate within the Palestinian community—in Beirut, Amman, London, the occupied territories, everywhere, in fact, where there were Palestinians—began to take place on the merits of such a state. Major PLO figures, especially in Europe, began espousing such a state, as well as the corollary necessary dialogue with Israelis. It was in the 1970s that Fatah figures like Sa'id Hamami, PLO representative in London, who were vociferous proponents of the two-state idea, were assassinated. Wa'el Z'eitar was assassinated in Rome, and Na'im Khader in Brussels. In spite of the bullets, however, the idea kept gaining strength and support within the Palestinian national movement. During its sixteenth session, in

Algiers in 1983, the PNC for the first time formally adopted a two-state solution. The route was admittedly circuitous, thus still reflecting the near-predominance of the rejectionist school of thought, and the PNC shied from explicitly endorsing dialogue with Zionists. But by endorsing what was then called "the Brezhnev Peace Document," as well as the 1982 Arab Fez peace plan, the PLO had in fact for the first time formalized its acceptance of a two-state solution. Still, by accepting the two-state solution but not endorsing dialogue with Zionists, the proceedings contained, to my mind, a gap between theory and practice—a gap which first revealed itself when the PNC refused to let Issam Sartawi be heard at the session, and through which the assassin's bullet that killed him in Lisbon later in the year was able to penetrate.

This gap between theory and practice was filled in during the PNC's seventeenth session, in Amman in 1986, when dialogue with Israelis became legitimized. But by then dialogue between Israelis and Palestinians had intensified on every level, and the Palestinian support for a two-state solution almost assumed an official character. True, opposition still existed, but so did support. Perhaps not so surprisingly, in view of the transformation that was taking place, but definitely not as widely well known, was yet another change which began to take shape from the early 1980s—namely, the PLO encouragement of the adoption of a civilian, nonviolent resistance strategy. Within the PLO, the "father figure" who provided encouragement for the development of this strategy was none other than Khalil al-Wazir, or Abu Jihad, who also fell before the bullets of an assassination squad in 1988. It may be true that he only envisaged this as a corollary strategy to complement the pursuit of military struggle against Israel, but it is equally true that his main faith was in the people of the occupied territories, and therefore in a strategy that was workable for them. The 1980s witnessed a conscious though slow evolution in the articulation and deployment of such a strategy, highlighted in the early part of the decade by substantial civilian action against certain Israeli measures (the introduction of the "Civilian Administration" and the struggle over the issue of "academic freedom") and developing later and significantly as joint Israeli-Palestinian action (the trigger being Israel's decision to expel a major Palestinian resistance figure, Abu Ali Shahin).

When the intifada first "officially" broke out in December 1987, there was a brief flashback to the pre-1970s political vision, inspired by a sense of euphoria and elation. However, this flashback did not last longer than a few weeks, and two major facts came back to full view and with full force: first, that the resistance strategy to be adopted was to be a civilian strategy; and second, that the scope of the political demand was to be the establishment of an independent Palestinian state alongside Israel, with East Jerusalem as its capital. In a sense, therefore, the intifada somehow constituted the powerhouse in which all the major transformations over the two previous decades in Palestinian strategy converged. It is against this perspective that plans for a civilian resistance strategy and for a declaration of independence emerged from the heart of the intifada itself. True, there was still opposition, but public support was becoming significantly more predominant.

So predominant, in fact, that the PNC was finally enabled to take its major step in November 1988, when it issued a Palestinian Declaration of Independence deriving its international legitimacy from the Partition Resolution of 1947, and when it also called for negotiations with Israel on the basis of UN resolutions, including Security Council Resolutions 242 and 338.

With this Declaration, the process of transformation became officially sealed. What was at first simply unthinkable, and later unacceptable, and later still acceptable only with great difficulty, had finally become accepted. The Palestinian national movement, embodied in the PLO, had finally and formally brought itself to recognize Israel, thus making an unprecedented official break with the past. Some reporters present at the historic session say that one very prominent PNC member, when asked why his eyes were full of tears at the announcement of the birth of a state, responded by saying that he was making his final farewell to Jaffa, his birthplace.

Indeed, the forty years since Israel's establishment in 1948, and since the beginning of the Palestinian diaspora, had constituted a tortuous self-searching journey in a political wilderness for the Palestinian nation. During this journey, many beliefs had to be shed, and in a sense there had to arise a new generation which was capable of confronting the challenge to Palestinian freedom that came to exist in Palestine in the form of the might of the nation of Israel.

Autobiographies—in this case the self-perception of Palestinians—may help to reveal the motivation behind certain acts or attitudes. However, it is personal military or power inventories, rather than morality or rights inventories, which determine national decisions and the political agenda. Crudely put, neither the Israelis nor the Palestinians would have wished the other side to be there. Israel would have preferred it if there were no Palestinians and if it could have therefore extended its sovereignty throughout the area from the river Jordan to the sea. Equally, Palestinians would have preferred it if there were no Israel and if a Palestinian Arab state could therefore have been established in that same region. But the two sides are there, and neither one of them is capable of abolishing the other altogether from its agenda. Israel's military capability enables it to forestall any possible decisive Arab military attack. But it does not enable it, except at a cost it cannot historically afford, to erase the Palestinian people from the map. And as long as the Palestinian people exist, especially those under Israel's control, then the dilemma outlined by Yehoshafat Harkabi, among others, will also exist: that either those Palestinians will be given their full political rights in the Israeli system, thus transforming the state into a non-Jewish democratic state, or they will be denied those rights, thus transforming the state into a non-Jewish apartheid state. Either way, Israel will cease to be a predominantly Jewish state. This dilemma will not be resolved through the influx of Soviet immigrants, although it may be pushed away further in time. Nor will it be invisible, either to Israelis themselves or to the international community, as the intifada has come to prove. Quite the contrary, the chances are that this dilemma will continue to be sharpened by the day, and the more immigration is relied upon to delay it, the more inescapable another dilemma becomes—namely, Israel's social and economic incapacity to absorb new immigrants. However one looks at it, the future Israel would be drawing for itself would be fraught with cumulative dangers, the kind of dangers Israel was created in order to avoid. Nor should potential Arab military capability be totally dismissed. If Israel can avoid concluding an acceptable peace settlement with the Arab people, it cannot avoid an ongoing state of conflict with them and the continuing specter of possibly sustaining heavy human damage, in spite of its strength.

It is through an appreciation of this inbuilt Israeli limitation that one can appreciate the strength of Palestinian bargaining power. Many Palestinians fail to see the Israeli limitation, and therefore their own strength. Looking simply at the weapons inventory, they conclude that any negotiation with Israel at this point will be one-sided, because Israel has the decisive upper hand. However, while it is true that the balance of power is tilted in Israel's favor, it is also true nonetheless that Palestinians possess a significant bargaining chip. Samir Sbeihat, a student leader whom I once had the privilege of teaching, and whom I considered a friend, and who was deported by the Israeli authorities following the outbreak of the intifada, put it to me like this: "Israel dominates the present, but Palestinians dominate the future. What is required, therefore, is an exchange. Something of the future which the Palestinians hold in exchange for something of the present which the Israelis hold." To my mind, this remains in essence the motivating force for any negotiation between Israelis and Palestinians, and I remember Labor Party leader Shimon Peres later echoing similar thoughts.

However, it is obviously a damage-limitation motivating force. In addition to it, there is a brighter side to negotiations—namely, the value itself of a peace treaty and the implications deriving from it. Both Israel and the Palestinians in a Palestinian state stand to gain from such a treaty. Positive human needs on both sides—the satisfaction of which ought to constitute the goal, after all, of political endeavor—can come to be addressed as priority items. If, furthermore, the proper economic system in the region is constructed, then leaps can be made in the joint advancements of all nations in the area. There is no reason why the Mediterranean region cannot advance closer as an economic unit to a newly emerging Europe and world order. After all, no one is under the illusion that a state can fulfill the positive human needs of the twenty-first-century human being. If national aspirations and fulfillment are appropriately addressed, then a smoother transition can perhaps be effected in the direction of the liberation from nationalism and from closed state structures.

A final word, I believe, needs to be addressed to the issue of PLO participation in negotiations. To my knowledge, there are various arguments that have been put forward against PLO participation in negotiations. I would like to take issue briefly with some of these arguments.

1. There are those who argue against PLO participation in negotiations because they believe that the PLO means quite simply a state for the Palestinians. Since they oppose a Palestinian state, therefore they oppose PLO participation. This argument has nothing to do with the PLO as such, and only indirectly relates to it through the idea of a Palestinian state. It follows that the proper context to address it in is the context of whether a state for the Palestinians is advantageous to Israel or not. I believe this work generally addresses this issue.

2. Sometimes the description "terrorist organization" is used in order to defend the submission that the PLO cannot be accepted as a partner in peace negotiations. There are two kinds of premises embedded in this argument, the first being that the PLO is indeed a terrorist organization. The second premise is rather less clear, and it may either be that terrorist organizations are excluded from historical deals or that they ought to be excluded from such deals. If it is the former, then this premise is obviously false, since history abounds with examples of treaties reached with individuals or groups and organizations that were once labeled "terrorists." If it is the latter—that is, that such organizations ought not to be dealt with—then this principle should be applied across the board—and it blatantly is not—so that the argument for its implementation in the case of the PLO would be valid. One must remember in this context that "organization" can apply to a nongovernment group as well as to a government. Secondly, however, perhaps a closer look should be taken at the very description of the PLO as a terrorist organization. While one cannot deny that certain PLO-affiliated groups or individuals have indeed participated in attacks against civilians, one cannot deny either that the PLO officially does not espouse such attacks and considers only military or strategic personnel or establishments to be legitimate targets. As such, and unless one were to deny the use of military means for the defense or attainment of legitimate national goals as acceptable (though undesirable) international methods all round, one can hardly be justified in singling out the PLO for such a restriction.

3. A third argument sometimes submitted is that the problem that needs to be addressed is that of the 1.7

million Palestinians in the West Bank and Gaza. Since the PLO is an external organization, representing (if at all) predominantly the diaspora sector of the Palestinian population, therefore there is no reason for it to be involved in negotiations. The argument here is based on the desire to drive a wedge between Palestinians in the occupied territories and those who are in exile. The implicit concern behind it is the fear that even if it wanted, Israel cannot address itself to the aspirations of the entire Palestinian community. However, it is unrealistic to expect that a properly constructed peace settlement can be achieved to the exclusion of the Palestinians who are in exile: first of all, they themselves (at the very least) would oppose it, and consequently, the role of the Arab world in absorbing at least part of their problem would be severely curtailed. Given this, it cannot be in Israel's interest to exclude the PLO.

An additional point that needs to be noted in this context is that "diaspora Palestinians" are not a different species of people, or more specifically of the Palestinian people. Very often, Palestinian families are split down the middle, with the first half having residence rights in the occupied territories and the second half being denied such rights. Some members of the PLO Executive Committee, and of other PLO organs, are deportees—that is, they are individuals who once had residence rights in the occupied territories but were expelled by the Israeli authorities. Therefore, it is highly unrealistic to expect that one half of the Palestinian community would agree to forgo the other.

Another aspect to this argument may stem from a limited appreciation of what is called the "Palestinian problem." Some people tend to have been inspired to support a settlement by events of the intifada, which they look upon as a purely West Bank/Gaza affair and which is a consequence of Israel's occupation of these areas in 1967. However, the Palestinian problem is the problem partly of territories which have been occupied, and it is also partly the problem of a people, a significant portion of which have been dispossessed of their land. In sum, it is the problem of a people who are denied a national homeland. Therefore, the only realistic way to address this problem is to address the Palestinian people as a whole, whether they live under Israeli rule or outside. There is no political vehicle through which to address this people except through the PLO, which is a common denominator of Palestinians wherever they happen to be.

4. Yet another argument one hears has to do with "representation." The question put here is: Does the PLO truly represent the Palestinian people? The answer usually given is that, since the PLO is not an elected body, therefore it cannot be representative. Here one must further add that quite often in anti-PLO propaganda it is claimed that the only reason for the PLO's continued political visibility and for the absence of any alternative is its use of intimidation and terror as a tactic to silence opposition. What I personally find distasteful in this part of the argument is its racist undertone— that the Palestinian people are constitutionally incapable of rising up against a tyrant. I believe that the intifada is a rebuff to this slight. However, to go back to the main argument, it is curious that it was never brought up in the context of, say, negotiating a deal with His Majesty King Hussein of Jordan. It is certainly not brought up in the context of Hafez al-Assad of Syria. Nor does it seem to stand in the way of not only negotiating deals with but more assertively supporting

the restoration to power of the Sabah family of Kuwait. Only in the case of the Palestinians does it seem to become a requirement.

Actually, the PLO welcomes elections. The PLO explicitly went along with the so-called elections plan proposed by the previous Israeli government under the premiership of Shamir, and it was Israel's own intransigence to U.S. efforts that caused that plan, and the coalition government that stood behind it, to collapse. Furthermore, when Israel in 1976 made its single effort at arranging municipal elections in the occupied territories, it is a well-established fact that all those who won did so on pro-PLO platforms. It is also a well-established fact that in all self-initiated and -arranged elections of active political bodies in the occupied territories (professional unions, labor unions, charity organizations, student unions, academic unions, etc.) there has been hardly any opposition to pro-PLO candidates. The only exception is the Islamic fundamentalist movement, which constitutes a significant force but is by no means a majority. Finally, in the only public opinion poll conducted on the issue (in 1986) by Australian Television, *Newsday*, and the local *al-Fajr*, it was revealed beyond doubt that the PLO commands the support of the overwhelming majority of the Palestinian people under occupation.

As for the PLO structure itself, members of the National Assembly (PNC) elect the Executive Committee, besides directly electing the chairman, the speaker, and the chair of the National Fund. PNC members are drawn from the constituent groups of the PLO as well as from elected organizations in various walks of life—women's groups, students, writers, etc.

In sum, therefore, although the PLO's various organs

are not directly elected by the Palestinian people, the PLO structure is still the closest possible approximation to what would be elected if the Palestinian people had the freedom to engage in democratic elections. In any case, insofar as representation as such is concerned, I do not believe that many Palestinians can be found who are opposed to the political program which the PLO espouses or to the national aspiration which the PLO embodies. Therefore, the argument to exclude the PLO from negotiations on these grounds seems spurious.

5. It is sometimes argued that the PLO should be excluded from the peace effort simply because it is not wholeheartedly committed to such an effort. The PLO would thus be a Trojan horse in any negotiations, torpedoing the process as soon as it began to bear fruit. Besides the countless well-known facts that refute this contention (the latest being the PLO's willingness to go along with Secretary of State Baker's attempt to get Israeli-Palestinian dialogue going in Cairo), there are countless little-known facts that also refute it. These facts concern the various efforts made through the years to initiate a serious dialogue between the PLO and Israel. I personally happen to have been a direct witness to and a participant in one such effort. The "Amirav affair," as it was called, began when Moshe Amirav, then a Likud Central Committee member, approached me in the early part of the summer of 1987 with the information that there is growing recognition within his party of the Palestinians as a people and of the PLO as their political interlocutor. Furthermore, he said he had some ideas about a possible settlement to discuss, which he thought might be supported by some of his col-

leagues, among whom he named highly placed Likud officials. After a lengthy series of meetings which also involved, on the Palestinian side, Faisal Husseini and journalist Salah Zuheike, a tentative draft was prepared to be presented to Chairman Arafat for his consideration. The whole effort finally broke down on the eve of a planned trip by Amirav to Geneva, where he was supposed to discuss this draft with Chairman Arafat, when he backed down at the last minute. I cannot presume to talk about the complexities at the Israeli end which caused Amirav finally to pull out—the repercussions later caused him to resign from his party—but the experience at the Palestinian end convinced me beyond doubt of the genuine interest of the PLO leadership in pursuing negotiations for as far as they can go.

6. Yet another argument is that the PLO cannot be trusted to "stick to its word." This is obviously not an argument but a statement. It is also a baseless statement, since no clear evidence exists that might be called upon to support it. In May 1990 the United States decided, following the failed Abul Abbas beach attack, to suspend dialogue with the PLO for not having kept its promise to freeze military activity. The PLO leadership was unable to take any measures against Abul Abbas, on the other hand, because of his contention that his target was military rather than civilian. Israel's claim was that the target was to have been a civilian target. Understandably, the PLO leadership could not, for lack of clear evidence, give more weight to Israel's claim than to Abul Abbas's claim. Naturally, the United States would have wanted no attacks, whether on military or civilian targets. But in the understanding of the PLO leadership,

the relevant promise related to attacks on civilian targets
only. Therefore, no clear case of a breach of promise
by the PLO could be established.

On the other hand, there is clear evidence suggesting
that the PLO does keep its promises. The only (indirect)
arrangement reached between Israel and the PLO concerned a cease-fire along the Lebanese border, in 1981.
The PLO diligently kept its promise to stop all incursions
into Israel from the Lebanese border. When this indirect
truce finally broke down, it was through Ariel Sharon's
invasion of Lebanon in 1982, inspired ostensibly by the
failed assassination attempt against Israel's ambassador
in London by an unknown, but certainly not a PLO,
assailant.

7. A more recent argument used against PLO participation stems from the position it adopted during the
Gulf crisis. It is claimed that since the PLO supported
Iraq, it has therefore lost all credibility as a negotiating
partner. Three points can be made here. First, the
PLO's right to negotiate on behalf of Palestinians is an
internal Palestinian issue, and has nothing to do with
the PLO's attitudes to world problems. Second, if "support for Iraq" is to be used as the litmus test for
prospective Palestinian negotiations, it is arguable that
very few of the Palestinians from the occupied territories
would pass this test. Therefore, this argument becomes
as good as an argument against negotiations and a
settlement in the first place. Third, there seems to be a
persistent Western refusal to understand the real position of the PLO and the Palestinians regarding the Gulf
crisis. The PLO support of Iraq never meant support
for the occupation of Kuwait or the usurpation of the
Kuwaiti people's right to self-determination. Rather, it
was a natural opposition to the U.N.'s legitimization of

war against Iraq as a means of restoring Kuwaiti sovereignty. Partly, this opposition was based on the Palestinian assessment that war would create more problems than it would solve; and partly, it was based on the assessment that in legitimizing the use of force against Iraq, the U.N. was being suspiciously selective about the implementation of the Security Council resolutions. These assessments seem as valid now after the conclusion of the war as they did before its outbreak. In any case, such arguments, or the emotions behind them, can hardly be viewed seriously as "disqualifications" for the role of negotiating a settlement between Israel and the Palestinians, represented by the PLO.

In contrast, there is a single but powerful argument for why the PLO should be included in peace negotiations. With the PLO, negotiations can get off the ground, and any subsequent settlement can be backed by a considerable political support system. Without the PLO, the chances for negotiations getting off the ground are so slim as to be practically nil, while the chances for anything afterward holding together would be nonexistent. Therefore, if peace is required, the PLO is necessary. (From the Palestinian point of view, if peace is not achieved, the PLO becomes even more necessary.)

Before closing my personal remarks there are some final words I would like to say. First, I hope that the effort I put into this work will not be of value only to academics or intellectuals, if that. This is not meant to underrate intellectuals and academics, but to express my deeper concern that the political reality of the region in which I live may be positively influenced. I daresay I would not have exerted the effort required if I did not have this hope. To me this is not an academic exercise but a life concern. Second, I know this work will create controversy among Palestinians as well as among Israelis. If I hope for anything in this context, it is that intellectual charity be exercised in considering the ideas and solutions discussed. What the reader should take into account is that this text is less a reflection of issues having to do with justice than it is a text reflecting pure interests. Third, I recognize that this work cannot be a blueprint for a negotiated settlement between Israelis and Palestinians. I hope, however, that its conclusion is "living evidence" that successful negotiations between Israelis and Palestinians are possible. Finally, this project is also proof that even after the successful conclusion of such negotiations, friendship between the negotiators themselves is possible.

Introduction

Since the Israeli-Egyptian peace treaty of 1979, the major change in the Israeli-Arab conflict has been a gradual reversion to its original dimensions: a conflict between Jews and Arabs over control of the part of the British Mandate west of the Jordan River, which Jews call the Land of Israel and Arabs call Palestine. For almost twenty years after 1948, the Arab states, while often pursuing their own interests, effectively acted as guardians of the Palestinian Arabs (henceforth called Palestinians) and their cause; for another decade, these states retained the leading role in the conflict with Israel. Arab states continue to provide sympathy and material assistance to the Palestinians and they retain some measure of influence over Palestinian actions, but it is only the Palestinians themselves who have both a direct existential interest in the future course of the conflict and the capacity to make authoritative decisions about its possible resolution. This development is similar to the transfer of authority on the Jewish side from externally based Zionist organizations and institutions to the Jewish community in Palestine (the Yishuv) during the 1920s and 1930s, and it is symbolized by the so-called Lebanon War of 1982 (the first predominantly Jewish/Israeli–Arab/Palestinian war since the Jewish-Palestinian confrontation which preceded the invasion of Israel by some of the Arab armies in 1948), the outbreak of the intifada in the West Bank and Gaza in 1987, and the Jordanian decision to abolish legal and administrative ties with the West Bank in 1988.

These three events have in effect re-Palestinianized the conflict by pushing the Palestinian people to center stage in the confrontation with Israel, thus reempowering them with the political mandate to seek ways to engage Israel in a negotiated settlement. The Palestinian cause, having been the charge of the Arab governments since the poor showing of their armies in 1948, came more and more to be a primarily Palestinian responsibility. In the face of the immovable reality of Israel, this change has meant a transformation of priorities, with the question of national identity gaining predominance over the retrieval of the totality of lands lost. This transformation is reminiscent of an older Zionist conflict between the more pragmatic and the more ideological schools of thought within the Yishuv. Just as practical considerations led Ben-Gurion at one crucial stage in the history of the creation of Israel to advocate accepting the compromise on land embedded in the various partition proposals in order to allow Jewish national identity to assume institutional existence in the form of a state, so modern developments affecting the Palestinian community have pushed the issue of manifesting their national identity to the forefront. As a result, the question is no longer simply the loss of a marginal piece of land by the collective Arab system; instead, it is now a central issue of the Palestinian people's need to save part of its ancestral territory in order to preserve and develop its national character.

Of course, this transformation has not been steady, smooth, or complete. Important regional manifestations of the conflict remain, especially an unresolved bilateral confrontation between Israel and Syria. There was a major Syrian dimension to the Lebanon War, and Syrian-Israeli tensions could easily lead to another round of armed hostilities. Moreover, the direct adversaries continue to derive various degrees and types of support from their respective cultural hinterlands, Israel from the world Jewish community, the Palestinians from the Arab and, to a lesser extent, Islamic worlds. Indeed, Arab governments' support for the Palestinian cause remains in many ways both a litmus test of their political legitimacy and a useful vehicle for the promotion of other regional or international objectives they may have. Iraq is the most salient example of an Arab state which has no common border or other kind of bilateral connection with Israel but nevertheless, after years of relative uninvolvement, again became intensely engaged in the Israeli-Arab conflict. The Iraqi invasion of Kuwait demonstrated that other conflicts in the region can spill over into the Israeli-Arab arena. Moreover, by posing as the most militant champion of the Palestinian cause and by threatening and then attacking Israel, Iraq was able, at least temporarily, to burnish its Arab credentials. It also diffused Israeli and international attention to the Palestinian dimension while reviving concern over the military dimension and the dangers of war inherent in Israel's relations with Arab states. Iraqi rhetoric and actions, far more than any recent element of Israeli-Palestinian relations, created an atmosphere of real crisis in the Israeli-Arab arena, and whatever its other consequences, this development reminded all concerned about the intimate linkage, indeed the mutual dependence, between the two levels of conflict. Security considerations alone (not to speak of all the other factors) mean that the Israeli-Palestinian conflict cannot be resolved without a fundamental improvement in Israeli-Arab relations; such an improvement depends on more than Israeli-Palestinian agreement, but it cannot begin to develop from less than a clear indication that the Israeli-Palestinian conflict is at least in the process of being resolved.

Consequently, the trend noted at the outset of this chapter remains relevant in this sense: the key to the overall Israeli-Arab conflict is still in its "communal" dimension—i.e., in the Israeli-Palestinian conflict. There are no impersonal forces of history to predetermine the outcome of this conflict. Theoretically, conflicts may end with the total submission of one side or the other. But there is nothing to indicate that either Israel or the Palestinians will, in the foreseeable future, have the power to impose their maximal aspirations on the adversary. Without a political settlement, it is more likely that the conflict will simply go on and on. Depending on changing circumstances, each side will be able to achieve or maintain intermediate objectives by inflicting pain and deprivation on itself and the other. The only thing that can be said with certainty is that a resolution of the conflict is impossible unless the minimal needs and desires of both sides are reasonably satisfied.

Even this is not very instructive, because minimal needs and desires are subjective, by their very nature.

Only the political process can reveal whether any subjective definition is shared by enough people on each side to allow leaders to take credible positions, and only negotiations can reveal whether the positions taken on each side overlap enough to make an agreement possible.

Theoretically, an agreement could be based on a wide variety of political relationships between Israel and the Palestinians. In practice, however, the "re-Palestinization" of the conflict means that an agreed settlement is highly unlikely unless it incorporates the principle of Palestinian statehood. There is near-universal consensus among Palestinians that a Palestinian state is a minimal requirement, although there are serious differences about the process by which this objective should be pursued, greater controversies about what commitments should be given in return, and even more serious conflicts about the future fabric of such a state. But regardless of these differences, the common denominator among Palestinians, barring some highly improbable change, will make a political settlement conditional on the creation of a Palestinian state.

However, all of the territory on which Palestinian aspirations focus is controlled by Israel, and if it is obvious why Palestinians should want a state, it is far less clear why Israelis should agree to concede one. In fact, Israel has consistently opposed such a state, and despite the intifada and changes in the official policy of the Palestine Liberation Organization (PLO), the majority of Israelis remain adamantly opposed to the so-called two-state solution. The reasons for Israeli attitudes include emotional attachment to the entire Land of Israel and the vested interests of settlers who might

be adversely affected. The predominant concern, however, appears to be national security in the broadest
sense of the term, meaning the fear that such a concession to Palestinians would not produce a real and
durable peace, but simply a less defensible border from
which the inevitable next war would have to be fought.

For some Israelis, sentiments or fears are so profound
that nothing will change them; in the absence of any
other alternatives (which is likely to be the case), they
will continue to prefer the status quo. Others may
perhaps change their position on a two-state settlement,
but only if they are persuaded that the deal is worthwhile—i.e., that it serves their larger national interests.
And they can be persuaded of that only if the settlement
includes certain provisions, particularly in the military/
security sphere, which are highly asymmetrical. Such
provisions might appear to Palestinians to be unfair,
hence a derogation of their rights, but if they are what
make possible the creation of a Palestinian state, then
they ultimately serve the larger national interests of the
Palestinians as well.

Whatever the contributions of outsiders may be, only
the Palestinians themselves can offer Israelis a vision of
the future that is more appealing than the reality of the
present, though even the most well-intentioned Palestinians will find it exceedingly difficult to do so. The
processes of attitude formation and change are complex
and murky. Leadership undoubtedly plays a vital role,
as do images and personal experiences. Rational argument is at best a minor factor, and even then only if it
proceeds from shared basic assumptions which are
themselves not necessarily rational. Consequently, authors of analytical studies should not expect to have

anything but the most marginal impact on the attitudes that underlie high policy. Still, the promise of even a marginal impact is enough to justify the effort.

The primary purpose of this study is to help educate interested publics in the Middle East and elsewhere about the possibilities and complexities of the two-state solution. This can best be done by bringing the discussion of the issue down from the level of cosmic meaning to the level of concrete concerns that need to be addressed and concrete problems that need to be resolved. The first task is simply to identify the agenda of issues and examine the interests and aspirations of Israelis and Palestinians. The second and more challenging one is to consider the extent to which mutually acceptable solutions are possible. In other words, we are laying out a map and attempting to plot a joint route.

The authors of this book are two independent scholars who do not claim to represent the prevalent opinions of their respective communities or presume to speak in their names. What we do claim is a familiarity with the concerns and feelings on each side and the belief that we can put forward informed personal judgments combining the feasible and the desirable. The gap between Israelis and Palestinians is probably wider than that separating the authors as individuals, so that even when we succeed in arriving at common positions, our agreement should not be understood to mean anything more than a belief that our positions should be considered seriously by Israelis and Palestinians. Sometimes, of course, we cannot agree, and we then refrain from putting forward a specific formula, indicating instead simply that the issue must be resolved through negotiations at some later date. On such occasions, we console ourselves with the knowledge that we have at least helped enrich the explanation, for those who are still perplexed, of the seemingly intractable nature of the conflict.

1

Security Arrangements

Whatever other reservations Israelis might have about a Palestinian state, they are almost unanimously concerned about the possible risks it presents for Israeli security. It matters little that a peace settlement involving the establishment of such a state would reduce the incentive of Palestinians and other Arabs to initiate a war sometime in the future; even if the psychological or political "need" for conflict is diminished, any weakening of Israel's defensive capability might make a military attack less dangerous, hence more tempting, hence more likely. If Israel looks weaker as a result of a political settlement, Arab decision makers might behave with less restraint during some political confrontation or even make a conscious choice in favor of war.

In principle, a substantial number of Israelis are prepared to withdraw from most of the West Bank and Gaza and agree to a Palestinian state in return for "true peace." But among the same group of people, many are highly skeptical that this would really be the peace to end all wars. This is not simply the result of Israeli insularity and congenital distrust of Arabs; most wars in most places have broken out between parties previously at peace. It will be a long time, if ever, before Israelis are convinced that war is simply unthinkable, and they will almost certainly continue to resist a two-state solution to the conflict unless they are convinced that it provides reasonable compensation, in the form of credible security arrangements, for any territory ceded in return for peace.

None of this is meant to imply that Palestinians do not also have security concerns. At present, their vulnerability stems largely from their condition of statelessness, but problems of state security may well arise following a settlement. A Palestinian state, for example, might be subject to military threats from other Arab states, and its independence or even its very existence might be threatened by the ascendancy of revisionist forces in Israel intent on undoing the work of that government which had agreed to a Palestinian state in the first place. There is, however, a basic asymmetry insofar as the implications of a two-state settlement are concerned: the Israeli territorial concessions that will make possible a two-state settlement mean the loss of geostrategic assets and the assumption of significant risks, whereas the Palestinians lose no material assets and do not run the risk of being worse off after a settlement than they are before one. It is this situational asymmetry, not a discriminatory perspective, that explains the specification of Israeli security requirements as the context within which Palestinian concerns must be addressed, and particularly the understanding that a Palestinian state cannot acquire the military capability to defend itself against most potential threats without simultaneously posing an unacceptable danger to Israel.

Most Arabs will argue that Israeli fears are exaggerated since Israel has the most powerful army in the Middle East, stronger than any potential Arab adversary and perhaps even than any conceivable coalition of Arab adversaries. Whatever the validity of this assessment, it is also true that, most of the time, most of Israel's army is either at home or at work in factories, farms, shops, and offices. Israel has too few people and too few resources to support a large permanent army. Instead, it has a militia; the bulk of the ground forces are reservists, and the power of the Israel Defense Forces cannot be brought to bear unless there is time to mobilize them.

The geostrategic importance for Israel of the West Bank is that its geography and topography provide this time. The dominant feature of the West Bank is a mountain ridge running like a spine down the center of the area. The mountain slopes gradually to the west, overlooking the coastal plain in which the bulk of Israel's population and industry are concentrated. To the east, however, the incline is fairly steep and is cut by only a few narrow axes along which heavy vehicles can move up from the Jordan Valley. Furthermore, the valley floor is only about 80 kilometers in length, whereas the Green Line represents a front of approximately 300 kilometers. In other words, the West Bank naturally shortens and fortifies Israel's eastern frontier.

As long as Israel retains control of the West Bank, it can take advantage of these features in two ways:

1. To maintain ground stations on the mountain peaks and operate information-gathering equipment in West Bank airspace in order to enhance early warning

of any war preparations east of the Jordan River (e.g., higher alert status of Jordanian forces, entry of Arab expeditionary forces into the East Bank); and

2. To entrust the initial defense to relatively small standing forces, because an invasion would have to begin by crossing a water obstacle (the Jordan River), move into prepared fields of fire, and then funnel heavy forces into the relatively few axes of advance to the west. The necessarily slower pace of the invasion would permit Israeli reserves to be mobilized and deployed for battle, either here or on other fronts. The West Bank is also a vital element in Israel's air defense; beyond the few extra minutes of flying time it imposes on attacking aircraft, it provides an ideal basing platform (on the peaks and eastward-facing mountain slopes) for long-range detection facilities and surface-to-air missile batteries.

In short, the West Bank is a critical force multiplier for Israel. If a political settlement transferred these military assets to Arab control with no constraints on their use, preparing against surprise attack would be prohibitively expensive, if not altogether impossible. Most of Israel's urban population and many of its air bases are within artillery range of the Green Line. In some sectors, the distance from the Green Line to the Mediterranean is less than 20 kilometers. To prevent a quick, coordinated thrust that could interfere with air force operations, disrupt communications and mobilization, and cut the country up into two or more separate pieces, Israel would have to keep very large forces in being at all times, meaning an intolerable strain on the economy, and it would have to adopt a "hair trigger" doctrine for the use of those forces which would be intolerant of any ambiguity at all concerning the actions of forces on the other side of the line.

Even if any areas evacuated by Israel were demilitarized, Israel would still be deprived of the military advantages it currently enjoys. Any subsequent remilitarization of the West Bank by Arab forces would have to be opposed lest Israel find itself in the same untenable position described above, but this would be far more costly in political terms and in casualties than if done by Israeli forces already present; a scenario posited by the Israeli side envisages that the race for the West Bank would begin with an Arab initiative, the local authorities and population would facilitate the movement of Arab armies while trying to hamper an advance by the IDF, and Arab moves, even though in violation of a peace treaty, would be viewed by the international community as actions by—or at the invitation of—the local sovereign, whereas Israeli moves would be seen as hostile infringement of a recognized border.

None of these risks would be intolerable to Israel if it were certain that any future military confrontation would involve only Israelis and Palestinians. Under most foreseeable circumstances, a Palestinian state acting alone could not mount a serious challenge to Israel, at least with conventional forces. The real strategic threat would come from some kind of Arab coalition in which the Palestinian state is an active partner, or at least an avenue of approach for other Arab armies.

If security were to be addressed solely on geographic grounds, it might be impossible to reconcile Israeli and Palestinian needs. However, it is not absolutely necessary for Israel to keep large military forces permanently in the West Bank or to deny a Palestinian state any defensive capability in order to avert the potential threats outlined above. But Israel must have an assurance that no other military force will be stationed there, along with the capacity both to monitor compliance with this assurance and to neutralize quickly any attempt to violate it. While meeting these conditions would involve some restrictions on the unfettered exercise of Palestinian sovereignty in Palestinian territory, many states voluntarily assume constraints on their freedom of action within the context of international agreements. Examples of this range from the Japanese constitution and the Austrian State Treaty to arms control agreements between the superpowers. Palestinian willingness to undertake such obligations would be the kind of persuasive evidence of peaceful intentions necessary to justify the residual risks of Israeli territorial concessions that will enable a Palestinian state to come into being.

One of these obligations would concern the foreign military relations of a Palestinian state: any peace settlement would have to preclude the temporary or permanent entry into Palestinian territory of foreign troops, except those (e.g., international observer forces) that might be mutually agreed on in the peace settlement itself.

Second, there would have to be limitations on the military establishment of the Palestinian state itself. Some minimal military capability would clearly be necessary, for symbolic purposes as well as to ensure internal security. By the same token, any Palestinian capability to disrupt Israeli mobilization schedules or interfere with an Israeli advance eastward in response to a crossing of the Jordan River by other Arab armies would be unacceptably threatening, in the sense that it would greatly improve the prospects of success for a coordinated campaign by an Arab coalition. It is possible to reconcile these conflicting requirements by means of limitations on the size, equipment, and deployment of Palestinian military forces, and the maintenance of a minimal, unobtrusive Israeli presence in the West Bank at least for some period of time until deeper structural changes in Middle Eastern politics and society had made a future war far less probable.

As far as Palestinian forces are concerned, the underlying principle would be that they waive the capacity to distract the IDF from its primary mission—foiling a possible invasion by other Arab armies. This would obviously mean a prohibition on any weapons enabling a Palestinian army to participate in combined offensive operations—i.e., tanks, artillery, and surface-to-surface missiles. But it would also imply a ban on equipment often classified as "defensive"—such as antitank missiles, antiaircraft missiles, and fortifications of any kind— which could be used to slow down an Israeli advance long enough for main-force units from other Arab states to secure vital strongpoints, especially the mountain ridge, in the West Bank. The basic mission of the army would be to enforce the domestic authority of the government, and for this mission, a force not exceeding three brigades (divided between the West Bank and Gaza in a ratio of 2:1) would suffice. This force would be equipped with personal weapons, armored cars, light mortars, and necessary communications and transportation infrastructure.

The same logic would require that any air force essentially be a public-safety agency, equipped with light patrol aircraft and helicopters appropriate for search-and-rescue operations, natural disaster relief, etc. The navy would be configured for similar missions (customs patrols, search-and-rescue, antismuggling tasks, etc.), without any heavy armaments or combat capability. Needless to say, the Palestinian state would be required to undertake not to develop or acquire any unconventional weapons—nuclear, chemical, or biological.

From the Palestinian perspective, any military buildup beyond the limits outlined here would in any event not be cost-effective, given Israel's military capabilities. The Palestinian state could not, by itself, raise an army capable of invading Israel or standing up to a major Israeli attack, and the historical record indicates that it would be illusory to depend on a coalition with Arab states to create that capability. Consequently, any investment in military forces beyond a certain point would be wasteful and counterproductive, and would be better allocated for economic development.

As far as any Israeli military presence is concerned, its main purposes would be to verify implementation of limitation agreements on forces and weapons, to maintain an early-warning capability against threatening military developments east of the Jordan River, and, if necessary, to enable Israel to conduct its primary defensive effort on the eastern slopes of the mountain ridge, but not to infringe on Palestinian sovereignty or otherwise provoke Palestinian sensitivities. Consequently, Israeli military installations should be located in specified security zones, agreed upon in advance and at a distance from population centers. The purpose of such installations, at least for a transitional period whose length depends primarily on the development of technological substitutes for physical presence, would be threefold:

1. To provide early warning, for which ground stations on some mountain peaks and reconnaissance overflights of the West Bank are necessary;

2. To prevent crippling first strikes by Arab air forces or vertical envelopment by air- or heli-borne Arab ground forces, for which anti-air defenses situated on the eastern side of the mountain crest are necessary; and

3. To slow any advance by heavy Arab ground forces while providing some mechanism to overcome Israeli political inhibitions against a large-scale use of the IDF in the West Bank, for which "trip wire" units near the eastern entrances of the roads leading up from the Jordan Valley are necessary.

Resupply of these facilities and rotation of personnel should be carried out at times and along routes (preferably away from population centers) coordinated with the Palestinian authorities, who would probably understand that any attempt to disrupt their orderly functioning would itself be interpreted in Israel as a kind of "early warning."

At the present time, Israel also makes use of the West Bank for training purposes, especially for the air force. It is not clear whether use of West Bank airspace for training purposes is absolutely indispensable, in the sense that other facilities are. If so, some agreement could presumably be reached on the degree and extent to which this practice would continue after a settlement. By the same token, the stationing of third-party—e.g., United Nations—personnel at ports of entry to observe compliance with the prohibition on imports of certain types of weapons could be reviewed after a transitional period.

If these security arrangements are incorporated into an Israeli-Palestinian peace agreement (along with the stipulation that they would continue to apply to the West Bank should the Palestinian state decide to associate or unify with some other political entity), Israel would have the ability to deal with a military threat emerging from or through the West Bank. In fact, this ability would further reduce the likelihood that such a threat would emerge. Even so, some of the arrangements might only be of a transitional character. For example, certain facilities or types of presence could be phased out as technological substitutes (e.g., highly capable satellite surveillance or other sensors, robotics, etc.) became available. Others might be viewed as outmoded if conclusive changes in Arab military capabilities take place as a result of changes in force posture, reductions in military expenditures, or arms-control agreements, or if peace becomes a normal state of affairs, institutionalized through refugee resettlement, multilateral cooperation, and force of habit, and the fear of war recedes.

While the kinds of security arrangements outlined above refer primarily to the geographical implications of a settlement for conventional military problems, they clearly do not constitute a comprehensive "security regime" for the region. For example, satisfying Israel's strategic needs with respect to the West Bank does not reduce or eliminate the dangers posed by long-range ballistic missiles carrying conventional or mass-destruction warheads (biological, chemical, or even nuclear); this reality was highlighted by recent events in the Gulf region. If the leadership of some Arab country were undeterred by the threat of retaliation and decided to attack Israel with such weapons simply in order to destroy lives and property, no Israeli military presence in the West Bank would make much of a difference. Problems of that type can only be dealt with, if at all, through some combination of arms-control and confidence-building measures and the development of defensive systems. On the other hand, the possibility that an opening missile strike might delay or prevent an Israeli response to a ground offensive from the east emphasizes the importance of prepositioned forces and equipment in the West Bank.

The introduction of more advanced technologies into the region does not necessarily mean that familiar concerns, including those related to geography, have become irrelevant. Indeed, it is conceivable that the proliferation of such technologies, by neutralizing the advantage in deep-strike capabilities that Israel traditionally enjoyed, may actually make a ground war appear to be a less risky proposition for Arab states with large armies but exposed rear areas. In any event, the inability of specific security arrangements to address all challenges does not nullify their value in dealing with some challenges, especially if those are the most probable and dangerous ones.

Second, any security regime should aim to accommodate Palestinian as well as Israeli concerns. While a Palestinian state cannot acquire the military strength needed to defend itself without deranging Israel's security requirements, its concerns can be addressed "extraneously." Specifically, what may be required are regional and even international agreements and guarantees designed to provide support in the event that Palestinian sovereignty was threatened or infringed without reasonable cause. As part of the peace agreement, Israel itself will obviously undertake not to use or violate Palestinian territory in an act of unprovoked aggression, and an international supervisory force can be established to monitor compliance with this commitment.

Third, for a security regime to be valid, it is not sufficient that its provisions cover only Israel and the Palestinian state. There will also have to be regional arrangements that will specifically take into account the security needs and concerns of other countries in this area. Agreements must be reached with these countries in order to "pacify" the region and to enhance the possibility of moving the entire area into a new phase of peaceful relations and cooperation. (Regional security arrangements are discussed in greater detail in Chapter 7, "Regionalization and Internationalization.") Such regional agreements will diminish the chances for conflict between Israel and other Arab countries, and thereby also diminish the risk that Palestinian territory will be violated either by other Arab armies or in the context of preemptive Israeli attacks.

Finally, the envisioned "security regime" must address a different kind of potential security problem—terrorism. The only conceivable post-settlement policy goal that could be promoted by terrorism would be the initiation of a cycle of escalation and a crisis atmosphere in which Arab states might be implicated. Since political considerations and security arrangements would militate against this, there would be little temptation on the part of any rational Palestinian government to sponsor terrorist operations against Israel. And even if that government were so inclined, it would probably be deterred by the threat of Israeli hot pursuit or retaliation. Moreover, there would probably be a less supportive environment among the Palestinian people as a whole for such operations.

Nevertheless, there is always a possibility that some individuals or groups might try to undermine the peace or discredit the Palestinian government by undertaking terrorist actions without its knowledge or approval. A Palestinian government will be committed to act against such elements, through an undertaking to prosecute or extradite arrested suspects and to share information with Israeli authorities. If a government is determined to implement these undertakings, its own intimate knowledge of various elements in Palestinian politics will give it a considerable counterterrorism capacity. But if the political will is lacking, there is little that security arrangements can do to rectify the situation.

It is important to note that the potential sources of terrorism are not limited to the Palestinian side. Many Jews will be vigorously opposed to the peace settlement, and some of them may resort to terrorism against Palestinian or Israeli targets in order to prevent its implementation or to undermine it afterward. Any obligations which the Palestinian state undertakes to prevent or punish terrorism must obviously apply to Israel as well, including sharing of information on the operation and movements of potential extremist groups.

In general, the Palestinian state can only achieve the security it will require through outside guarantors and a series of intricately worked out treaties and agreements to which the international community must be a party. Such agreements, treaties, and guarantees must include clearly predefined sets of possible penalties and punitive courses of action aimed at any parties which violate Palestinian sovereignty and security. In most cases, Israel's determination to exclude other forces from the West Bank will deter potential threats from Arab countries. On the other hand, the prospect of Arab and international sanctions and domestic upheaval would almost certainly deter Israel, which had already taken the agonizing decision to withdraw, from undertaking an invasion or major violation of Palestinian frontiers for any but the most vital of reasons, such as a major buildup of potentially hostile forces. Although this system of balances would go far toward ensuring Palestinian security, it would not preclude the possibility of collusion between Israel and some neighboring Arab states. To deal with that sort of threat, the Palestinians would have to rely on internationally sponsored agreements.

2

The Demarcation and Meaning of Borders

As a general principle, the importance of borders is inversely related to the nature of relations between neighboring states. Relations of tension, hostility, and mutual avoidance usually mean that political borders physically separate societies and engage the emotions of ordinary citizens and the attention of military planners. By contrast, relations of institutionalized peace and intense human and economic interchange may cause national borders to become little more than a minor administrative inconvenience. But neither the placid normalcy that characterizes U.S.-Canada relations nor the even more advanced integration likely to emerge in Europe after 1992 can completely eliminate the significance of borders. At the very least, political demarcation lines indicate the scope of legal systems and of government authority. They frequently have economic implications (e.g., tax codes and social benefits), and in the context of the Middle East as far into the future as one can project, they will also be of military significance. Consequently, the placement of those borders, notwithstanding the expectation of normal, peaceful relations between Israel and the Palestinian state, will not be an inconsequential matter.

We are unable to agree on a precise demarcation line and therefore confine ourselves to the overall principles which we believe should guide Israeli and Palestinian negotiators on this issue. There is no prominent physical feature, such as a river, which suggests itself. Nor is there any clear demographic dividing line. In the absence of such criteria, the most obvious point of departure should be political/historical. From this perspective, the most salient line is the 1949 Armistice line; although it was never recognized as an international border or consecrated by any peace agreement, it did separate Israel from Arab territory for almost twenty years before 1967 and it retained administrative and sociological significance thereafter, notwithstanding the presence of hundreds of thousands of Arabs in pre-1967 Israel and the subsequent settlement of tens of thousands of Jews in the West Bank. Moreover, the territories beyond the Armistice line—the West Bank and Gaza—are the obvious territorial focus of UN Security Council Resolutions 242 and 338, the most widely accepted principles for the settlement of the Israeli-Arab conflict.

Resolution 242, passed in November 1967 following the war, emphasizes the inadmissibility of the acquisition of territory by war, and affirms that the establishment of a just and lasting peace in the Middle East should include the application of two principles: withdrawal of Israeli armed forces "from territories occupied in the recent conflict" and "termination of all claims or states of belligerency and respect for and acknowledgment of the sovereignty, territorial integrity and political independence of every State in the area and their right to live in peace within secure and recognized boundaries free from threats or acts of force." Whereas Resolution 242 did not specify that negotiations between the conflicting parties should be a prelude for such withdrawal, Resolution 338, passed in October 1973, called upon the parties to implement the provisions of Resolution 242 and, concurrently with the cease-fire, to initiate negotiations "aimed at establishing a just and durable peace in the Middle East."

The main difference between these two resolutions, therefore, lies in the "bartering" or "quid pro quo" context for Israeli withdrawal: Resolution 242 made no specific reference to negotiations (though it did call for the appointment of a Special Representative to establish and maintain contacts with the states concerned) and this created some basis for the Arab assessment that the resolution (and especially the "withdrawal" provision) would somehow be implemented without negotiations; Resolution 338, reflecting changing circumstances, made any withdrawal virtually conditional on a negotiated peace treaty. What was implicit in 242 was thus made explicit in 338. In both cases, however, the clear international signal to the conflicting parties was that peace must be predicated, among other things, on Israeli withdrawal "from territories occupied in the recent conflict."

Throughout the years, these two resolutions have come to acquire a strong diplomatic standing, having been incorporated into almost every major international proclamation concerning the Middle East conflict. Their acceptance by the PLO was an essential prerequisite for the initiation of a U.S.-PLO dialogue, and prior to PLO acceptance in 1988, many Israeli leaders also stated that one of the obstacles to negotiating with the PLO was the latter's refusal to recognize these two resolutions. In short, these resolutions came to be "key terms" in any serious plan to establish peace in the region.

Even so, they are not totally without ambiguity. In particular, a persistent difference in interpretation has attended the term "territories" in Resolution 242, with the Arab side insisting that it refers to all of the territory occupied in June 1967 and the Israeli arguing that it refers only to some part of that territory. However, any ambiguity that exists in the wording of the Resolution was deliberate, since it would otherwise not have passed. Indeed, previous attempts to stipulate withdrawal from "all the territories" or even "the territories" had been unsuccessful. It is therefore clear that Resolution 242 does not oblige Israel to withdraw to the 1949 Armistice line. On the other hand, since the territories referred to in 242 were previously delineated by the so-called "Green Line," that line logically forms the basis from which any negotiations over borders must proceed, and the outcome should reflect a variety of other factors, as well.

Strictly speaking, there should be no need for border adjustments on security grounds if Israel's security requirements are met in accordance with the ideas outlined in Chapter 1 ("Security Arrangements"). However, in a generally favorable negotiating climate, certain other considerations may bear on this issue, particularly geographic and demographic anomalies. The most prominent example is the so-called Latrun Salient, which includes a small swatch of territory (several square kilometers) surrounded by a belt defined as "No-Man's-Land" in the Armistice agreements. The main Jerusalem–Tel Aviv highway runs through this salient just north of the Latrun monastery, and several Jewish settlements have been built in and near this area in the "Jerusalem Corridor" (both in No-Man's-Land and just over the Green Line in the West Bank).

The formal incorporation of some parts of this area into Israel, while allocating other parts to Palestinians, would be an example of minor territorial adjustments which do not reflect the weight of conquest but which satisfy the needs and aspirations of one side while causing minimal collective or individual disruption to the other. Farther afield and in a slightly different context, some demographic or urban anomalies may provide other reasons for possible border adjustments. For example, there are some Arab villages which are divided by the Green Line (e.g., Baqa, Barta'a) or situated just next to it on the Israeli side (e.g., Ibtin, Mukeibilah) whose inhabitants might, by the terms of a peace agreement, be offered the chance to decide themselves to which state they would prefer to belong. Conversely, the same principle could be applied to some of the Jewish settlements just across the Green Line. This choice could also be offered to the town of Rafah, which is divided between Egypt and the Gaza Strip.

While border adjustments of this sort may be appropriate in certain specific localities, they cannot provide a comprehensive solution to the problems of demographic intermingling, economic interaction between the two states, or the fact that two regions of the Palestinian state will be physically separated. It is therefore necessary to give as much attention to the character or "porosity" of the border as to its location. In general, it is reasonable to assume that the greater the porosity of the border—i.e., the more freely people, goods, and capital can move across it—the less rigidity there need be in negotiating its exact location.

This is of obvious relevance to the situation of villages or towns that may continue to straddle a border line, and, in the most extreme case, of Jerusalem (where any demarcation lines will, to a large extent, be more imaginary than real). Of course, Barta'a is not Jerusalem, but even in the former case, reason demands that any dividing line which might remain in place must be deprived of as much meaning or content as possible. This would mean allowing as much porosity as possible: free movement of persons, goods, and capital. It would also mean a highly advanced system of translatable, if not integral, legal codes. Both the porosity as well as the "translatability" will allow for a maximization of normalcy in social and economic affairs. For example, nationals of one state could own and use property even if it happens to fall within the sovereign territory of the other state, and the appropriate legal system (or translatable legal systems) can be elaborated which will allow for two-directional litigation procedures. This can be achieved through any number of possible methods, including the establishment of Higher Joint Courts of Law which can function as ultimate reference points for adjudication in cases of conflict or claims which involve nationals from the two states. In any case, mutual legal agreements have to be reached over a wide range of issues, including traffic regulations and violations, trade regulations and violations, and other areas of civic activity. The main point to be emphasized is that the more a border line dividing a village or town is impermeable, the more it will be a bone of contention. Conversely, greater permeability will make agreement easier to reach. It is true that porosity or permeability will mean a highly complex system of human relations and affairs, but it should be possible to devise the legal codes and regulations that are capable of embracing such a system, thus making the law a reflection of human needs.

In fact, these underlying principles should ideally be applied to the Israeli-Palestinian border along its entire length. In this sense, the border would have different levels of significance for different dimensions of relations: it would be most salient (or impermeable) in the political sense, somewhat less so in legal terms, perhaps even less so with respect to economics and trade, and of minimal practical significance from a military point of view.

A peace treaty between Israel and the Palestinian state will undoubtedly unleash development and investment opportunities for the two sides which are totally unthinkable today. Conversely, economic prosperity in the two states and the increase in the level of advantageous interdependence between them will reinforce the state of peace that will exist, making it more stable and durable. A joint target should therefore be to provide the conditions under which the Palestinian state will be able to develop its economy and to develop a mutually beneficial system of economic relations between the two states.

Paradoxically, this will entail the partial dismantling of the existing economic relationship between the West Bank/Gaza and Israel. This relationship has for the most part been one-sided since 1967, with the West Bank/Gaza territory constituting an export market for Israeli products (90 percent of all goods and services consumed by Palestinians in this territory have come either from or via Israel, leaving the territory with a perennial trade deficit of some $300 million annually) and a source of relatively cheap labor (numbering approximately 120,000 workers). This relationship resulted in improved standards of living but not in economic development; the West Bank and Gaza population, generally denied the possibility of developing their own infrastructure and making unfettered use of their land or water resources, grew largely as an adjunct, dependent economy.

Although complete economic separation from Israel would be neither prudent nor possible, a major priority should nevertheless be to reformulate the relationship. One possible way of doing so, at least in the initial stages, would be to provide partial "protection" for emerging Palestinian industries from the competitive and established foreign producers. However, such measures should take into account the benefits to be derived from border permeability and more generally from joint ventures and projects. Tourism, for example, is an area where regional interdependence would be both necessary and beneficial, and where the benefits derived from cooperation between the two states would be mutually advantageous. This benefit would obviously be enhanced by wider regional cooperation and freer access across borders. Once the Palestinian state's airport (in Kalandia, north of Jerusalem) begins functioning, agreements can be worked out for tourists to use either airport for domestic or international flights, and the more open the border, the easier it would be to handle this tourist traffic.

Cooperation will also be enhanced if the Israeli shekel and the new Palestinian currency are considered legal tender in both countries, or at least if the two currencies are freely convertible. In such a state of affairs, the possibilities of joint ventures become more obvious, in areas ranging from financing institutions to law offices.

Energy is another possible area of major cooperation, especially if the Dead Sea is to be utilized as a source of solar energy. Actually, the development of the Dead Sea in whatever direction would have to be closely worked out with the agreement of Jordan as well as Israel and Palestine. Yet another area of coordination, if not joint activity, is transport. Rather than curtail the process of integration of the road system as it has evolved since 1967, the further development of this integrated system would facilitate the flow of goods and people between the two states, as well as to and from the rest of the Middle East. The transport network can be further improved through the development of a railway system. Such a project would provide employment both in the construction/reconstruction stage and in routine operation and maintenance, but it would also open up outlying areas, encourage the establishment and growth of industries in such areas, provide cheap and easy travel, and, perhaps most important, take advantage of the region's unique geostrategic position in the Middle East as a major "crossroads" for the flow of trade between countries in the region.

Reactivation of the line through Gaza would be a useful adjunct to the port there and would provide a considerable boost to the Gaza economy. A railway connecting the West Bank and Gaza (perhaps by linking up with the existing Lod-Jerusalem line) would be able to cope with the large volume of traffic that might flow to and from the Gaza port, and it could also be extended westward, permitting revival of the rail service that existed between Israel/Palestine and Egypt before 1948.

In general, therefore, the benefits that would accrue

from joint ventures and the development of coordinated transport and other infrastructural systems—in addition to the practical necessities of joining up divided sovereign territories or providing access to such territories— all call for a maximum degree of porosity or permeability across borders. However, some bottom line on the Israeli as well as on the Palestinian side might be considered prudent—on the Israeli side perhaps to protect the Israeli market from a flood of cheap commodities from the Arab world (either directly or through the Palestinian state), and on the Palestinian side in order to protect the production of at least those commodities that might seem to be nationally essential. In particular, it should be noted that in a totally open market system, Arab labor might be tempted by higher Israeli wages, thus raising labor cost per unit of production of a commodity in the Palestinian state, thus making this commodity less competitive against similar or substitute Israeli products. Political measures to interfere with such market forces usually prove to be destructive, and the free movement of labor and capital would ultimately work to the economic benefit of consumers and producers in both states. At the same time, both sides will have certain political imperatives with respect to the pace and direction of their economic development, and a way must therefore be devised to synthesize the two requirements—maximum market interaction and the protection of some goods or services. Obviously, common sense would have to prevail, as it would be illogical for the Palestinian state to use scarce water resources for the production of, say, strawberries (which are highly water-dependent) when it can buy those from Israel (perhaps at a specially reduced rate in return for aquifer agreements). In any event, whatever economic development measures are adopted by either state must not be specifically and uniquely directed against the other. To the extent that Israeli-Palestinian economic relations are not preferential, they must at least not be discriminatory, in terms of either tariffs or nontariff impediments to free trade.

3

The Refugee Problem

Palestinians view the "refugee problem" as the heart of the Israeli-Arab conflict, the anchor of their collective memory and political motivation. From their perspective, the issue does not concern just the 1.5 million Palestinians scattered in refugee camps throughout the West Bank, Gaza, and the Arab world; nor even the 2 to 3 million other Palestinians who, while not living in refugee camps, still feel that they are forcefully being prevented from returning to their homeland. Instead, Palestinians see it as the very essence of the Arab-Israeli conflict, and any settlement which does not directly address this problem is therefore inconceivable. By inference, no such settlement can be reached if the exiled Palestinian population is excluded from the negotiating process through the exclusion of the PLO.

On the other hand, it is equally inconceivable that Israel will agree to the return of Palestinians to their original homes or those of their parents, even in the context of a peaceful settlement. To do so would be to undermine the Jewish character of the state—i.e., to contradict Israel's very raison d'être.

A settlement is therefore possible only if the Palestinians can somehow transcend almost completely the central reference point in their national memory and instead focus on replacing a tragic past with a hopeful future. How can this be done? What are the questions that have to be addressed and resolved? In particular:

1. What will happen to Palestinians now living in refugee camps in the Arab world?

2. What about all the other Palestinians, refugees and nonrefugees alike?

3. Will there be any limitations on Palestinian immigration to the new state? If so, who will be empowered to set them?

Refugee Camp Residents

For purposes of the following discussion, Palestinians are divided into two categories: refugee-camp residents and those who are not camp residents. The latter may be either registered refugees who do not live in camps or nonrefugees.

Although the United Nations Relief and Works Agency has sometimes been suspected of overestimating the actual numbers, it provides the only consistent series over many years and the following figures are drawn from UNRWA data. In 1988, Palestinian refugee camps were scattered around four main regions: (a) Gaza and the West Bank (28 camps housing approximately 350,000 refugees); (b) Jordan (10 camps with about 210,000 refugees); (c) Syria (10 camps holding about

75,000 residents); and (d) Lebanon, where an estimated 150,000 refugees live in 13 camps, some of which are now in a state of physical disrepair.

Palestinian residents of refugee camps in Arab countries are more likely than those who are not in camps to opt for residence in a new Palestinian state. Partly because of their economic conditions, they are both more politicized as a community and less tied to their current countries of residence. Of course, many of them will be equally unexcited about the prospect of living in the West Bank or Gaza; their attachment is to the homes and villages that they left in 1948. On the other hand, there will be a large group, especially from Lebanon and Syria, who will settle for a new home and for new prospects in the Palestinian state. As an integral part of any real settlement to the Palestinian-Israeli conflict, a serious effort must be made to terminate the phenomenon of refugee camps and the suffering of the Palestinians who live in them. This means that host countries must be prepared to absorb into their respective political systems Palestinians who choose to remain where they are; this means offering them citizenship and full political rights, while in no way detracting from any rights or privileges that such Palestinians may enjoy in the Palestinian state. By the same token, the new Palestinian state must prepare itself to accommodate a possible influx of perhaps three-quarters of a million newcomers, most of them from refugee camps. But whatever individual Palestinians choose to do, the two options—taking up citizenship in an Arab country and settling in the Palestinian state—must never be seen as mutually exclusive. Instead, the Palestinian state must at all times be to Palestinians what Israel is to the Jewish people—namely, a state for them all, wherever they may be.

Other Palestinians

Of the Palestinians who were displaced from their homes or born to parents in this category, approximately 1,434,000 are registered refugees but do not live in camps. In addition, there is an unknown number who are not registered with UNRWA as refugees. Finally, there is a population of Palestinian emigrants which has moved abroad for economic or other personal reasons.

The largest number of these Palestinians are in Jordan, where they enjoy Jordanian citizenship, but there are many in other countries, particularly in the Arab world (Saudi Arabia, the other Gulf states, Libya, and, to a lesser extent, also Syria, Lebanon, and Iraq). The majority either were born in these countries or have spent most of their productive lives there and have succeeded over a period of ten to forty years in carving out for themselves a comfortable standard of living. Nevertheless, they are generally denied citizenship in their host countries. As a result, they have not yet been able to enjoy the full potential of those countries or even a basic sense of security.

In some cases, as in Kuwait (assuming the decline of anti-Palestinian sentiment) and the other Gulf countries, citizenship would make it possible for Palestinian employees to enjoy the fruits of their labor after retirement and to bequeath social and economic benefits and residency rights to their children. In many cases, the acquisition of citizenship would also mean increased business opportunities, such as the right to set up a private business without having to share profits with a "national" or find a "sleeping partner." For a variety of reasons, many Palestinians, both refugees and non-refugees, will prefer to remain in their current countries of residence (1.3 million in Jordan, 0.5 million in the Gulf countries, 0.5 million in Syria/Lebanon, and 200,000 in other places).

Of course, internal economic and political considerations of Arab host countries will affect their willingness and ability to absorb additional Palestinians or extend citizenship to those already there. In some cases, these countries of residence will require help to provide the "new citizens" with the appropriate conditions and rights necessary for their absorption; in all cases, the need to involve Arab countries in the process of resettlement and reconstruction means that they must play an integral part in the peace process and endorse any political settlement.

Like the camp residents, these Palestinians should be free to opt for citizenship in their host countries without prejudicing or detracting from their rights in the Palestinian state, and this provision should also apply to Israeli Palestinians, some of whom may wish to hold Palestinian as well as Israeli citizenship. But whatever the preferences of individuals, the Palestinian state must be ready to provide citizenship to each and every Palestinian who desires it. If Palestinian options are diversified in this fashion, the result would almost certainly be a climate of opinion more conducive to compromise.

Resettlement in the State: Demographic Ramifications

About 1.7 million Palestinians now live in Gaza and the West Bank (including East Jerusalem). With an estimated influx of perhaps 750,000 to 1 million newcomers or returnees, and a natural growth rate of approximately 3 percent, the new Palestinian state could well have around 3.5 million inhabitants by the end of the century. This projection may raise a number of questions about the economic capacity of the state to sustain its population, as well as about the overall demographic balance between Arabs and Jews in Mandatory Palestine west of the Jordan River. Both questions are of strategic significance and will undoubtedly be raised during any negotiation process. In particular, the main questions to be addressed will be these: Will an economically unstable and overpopulated Palestine constitute an irredentist element in the region? And will the overall demographic picture, taking into account both Israel's Palestinian population and Palestine's newcomers and returnees, somehow constitute a threat to Israel's existence as a Jewish state?

In principle, the issue of demographic balance should not be allowed to enter into the negotiating calculations as a substantive issue of overriding importance. In regional terms, Israeli Jews constitute a small minority in an overwhelmingly Arab area; within the narrower confines of Israel/Palestine, there is no certainty, despite the large-scale influx of Soviet Jewish immigrants, that Jews will retain a substantial numerical majority through the coming decades. Therefore, if the demographic picture is viewed in racial or religious terms, "conservative" positions with regard to Palestinian immigration (into the Palestinian state) will probably be raised during negotiations, even though externally imposed constraints on migration, unlike security constraints, will not appear reasonable and are unlikely to be accepted by Palestinians or supported by anyone else.

On the other hand, a Palestinian state suffering from

acute overpopulation and economic distress will undoubtedly be unstable politically. This would be a threat
not only to Israel, since it could provoke a chain of
regional developments leading to renewed conflict, but
also to the Palestinian state. Consequently, it may be
both necessary and desirable to concentrate on an
instrumental approach that treats the issue from the
perspective of potential economic growth in the entire
region.

A Palestinian state in the West Bank and Gaza cannot aspire to be economically independent or self-
sustaining, regardless of whether its population is 1.7
million or 3.5 million. Any realistic assessment of a
Palestinian state's potential suggests that it will have to
be incorporated into a larger orbit or system if it is to
survive economically. Therefore, the key element here
is not whether such a state can be economically independent, but rather how this state, along with its neighbors, can form an economic unit that will be of benefit
to all of them. The demographic element must be
regarded as a *given*, along with such other elements as
the natural resources of the entire area and the need
for economic cooperation and integration. What must
be sought is the right formula for cooperation and
integration which will make the regional economic
system effective enough to permit each of its members
to prosper.

Although "technical" arguments are sometimes raised
against the admission of perhaps 750,000 Palestinians
into the new state, it should be noted that by 1985
Israel's own Higher Planning Committee had, according
to the 1986 report of the West Bank Data Project,
already laid out plans to accommodate in the West Bank
more than 500,000 settlers, in addition to those already

living there and in the Gaza Strip. It is not clear that those plans had any basis in reality, but to the extent that they were at all well founded, the absorption of Palestinian newcomers by a Palestinian state would be technically easier, given the national homogeneity involved and the availability of contiguous urban development zones, many of which have not been exploited because of severe Israeli restrictions since 1967. In any event, the capacity of the Palestinian state to absorb newcomers cannot be determined except in the context of certain assumptions about minimally acceptable standards of living and the availability of foreign assistance, and these issues are political and sociological rather than technical.

The major problem in this context, however, will be the resettlement of refugees in the Gaza District. Gaza has one of the highest population densities in the world, over 1,500 people per square kilometer (in the West Bank, by contrast, the figure is about 160, and in Israel, about 220). Almost half of Gaza's current population are refugees, of whom 250,000 live in 8 refugee camps. The entire region is only about 40 kilometers long and 6 to 12 kilometers wide, but in some refugee camps, such as Shati (Beach Camp), more than 42,000 are crammed into an area of only about one square kilometer. Moreover, Gaza's rate of natural increase is extremely high, about 4 percent per year. Given these realities, it is conceivable that Palestinian negotiators, basing themselves on the 1947 Partition Plan, may request Israeli territorial concessions in this sector in order to relieve population pressures.

This may be one approach, but even if it were adopted, it would not make a substantial difference given the dimensions of the population problem. To

produce a "normal" population density (e.g., like Israel's) by adding territory, one would have to add over
3,200 square kilometers to Gaza—i.e., to increase its
territory ninefold. Moreover, it is inconceivable that
Israeli negotiators would agree to such a request. Consequently, the most realistic approach for dealing with
the population problem is one that combines local
economic development with the removal of obstacles to
the movement of Gazans. In any event, such movement
to the West Bank will be natural within the context of
a single state.

Naturally, whatever the eventual population of the
new state, large amounts of capital investment will be
needed to ensure economic and therefore political and
social stability. A suitable model will ensure the availability of housing and employment opportunities, as
well as medical and educational facilities. Whatever the
case, the guideline for refugee resettlement should be
the creation of a state of affairs which, while by definition
not a reconstruction of pre-1948, is nevertheless appealing enough to persuade a people which has clung
to its past to let it go in favor of a brighter future.

The Right of Return

The United Nations General Assembly passed a resolution in 1948 (Resolution 194 III) which established a
Reconciliation Commission for Palestine. Paragraph 11
of the resolution stipulated that "refugees wishing to
return to their homes and live at peace with their
neighbors should be permitted to do so at the earliest
practicable date, and that compensation should be paid
for the property of those choosing not to return and

for loss of or damage to property which, under principles of international law or in equity, should be made good by the Governments or authorities responsible . . ." Most of the 1948 refugees have since died, but if the provisions of the resolution were extended to their descendants as well as to the survivors and their descendants, then its application would automatically mean the de-Judaization of Israel (since a large proportion of the approximately 2.2 million registered refugees would prefer to return rather than be compensated).

It is therefore impossible to implement Resolution 194 en masse, and this reality was implicitly recognized by the PNC when it approved the Palestinian Declaration of Independence on November 15, 1988. That declaration is predicated on UN Security Council Resolution 181 of 1947, which called for the partition of Palestine into a *Jewish* and an Arab state, and the acceptance of the former logically precludes the implementation of the "return" component of Resolution 194. However, the Palestinians will probably want to preserve the possibility of the admission to Israel of individuals whose personal circumstances are of a special nature, and Israel should be prepared to entertain applications on a case-by-case basis on humanitarian grounds.

On the other hand, the compensation component of the resolution must be given a weight which is in inverse proportion to that of the actual return component. This may be done in any number of possible ways. An international body of assessors can be set up to evaluate private Palestinian properties, as well as public lands and properties that were utilized by Palestinians, and this evaluation can include price adjustments and whatever other factor that may be deemed necessary. A possible next step is to balance this value against the cost of resettlement of Palestinians in the new state or elsewhere, and perhaps even the value of Jewish properties in Arab countries which were illegally confiscated by the governments in those countries. Individuals who do not make use of the resettlement program may receive direct compensation. As for individuals who do make use of the program, any balance over and above resettlement costs should be divided proportionally among all recipients of compensation. Even a nominal disbursement of financial compensations in this context may be of important psychological value and could facilitate a definitive political contract between the two nations, but a comprehensive program would be extremely costly and would depend on the active participation of the international community.

4

Settlements

The two major parties in Israel disagree about the aim and role of settlements in the West Bank/Gaza, and the settlement movement developed differently under Labor (1967–77) than under the Likud (1977–84) and National Unity governments (1984–89 and 1989–90). Objectively, however, the settlement movement has consistently worked to the disadvantage of one ethnic population and the advantage of another. This has been the effect of a highly sophisticated system of land confiscations, the creation of an independent infrastructure (roads, electricity, water, telecommunications), and the assumption of control over the area's water resources.

These measures and other complementary policies have throttled the capacity of the Palestinians to develop themselves. And although the most immediate restrictions have been on the use of land and water (agricultural and urban development), the indirect economic effects have been far-reaching.

Moreover, from a purely practical point of view, the hostility shown by settlers to Palestinians and Palestinian rights implies that their continued presence in a Palestinian state would necessarily be a destabilizing factor in a situation crying out for the reduction of instability and the defusing of conflict. In any case, Palestinians would not agree to perpetuating the present status of the settlements. But even if an Israeli government agreed to evacuate the settlements and forcibly return their inhabitants to Israel proper, which is virtually inconceivable, the very announcement that it had done so would itself create new instabilities and conflicts that would prevent any attempt to implement such an agreement. Therefore, certain concrete questions about the status of Jews in a Palestinian state have to be addressed in order to find a political formula that might command sufficient support on both sides. The main question is: What are the conditions under which Israeli Jews will be allowed to live in a Palestinian state?

Brief Historical Survey

In the early years of the Israeli occupation, Labor governments made use of Article 52 of the Hague Convention, which allows an occupying force to seize lands "for the needs of the army of occupation." According to a 1985 study by Usamah Halabi, Aron Terner, and Meron Benvenisti entitled "Land Alienation in the West Bank," Israeli authorities requisitioned 46,680 dunams of privately owned land "for military purposes" between 1968 and 1979. In fact, most of the area was ultimately used for the construction of civilian settlements, including Matityahu, Neve Tzuf, Rimonim,

Shiloh, Bethel A, Bethel B, Kokhav Hashahar, Alon Shvut, Elazar, Ephrat, Har Gilo, Migdal Oz, Gitit, Yitav, Kiryat Arba, and Kadum.

Using the same "military cover," the authorities also declared 1,106,640 dunams "closed areas." Strictly speaking, a closed military area is not used for civilian purposes, but the same study claims that the status of many of these areas was subsequently changed to requisitioned areas and state lands, thus enabling the authorities to use them for settlement purposes. An additional 38,000 dunams along the Jordanian border were similarly closed between 1967 and 1980 and then released for cultivation by Israeli settlers.

In addition to confiscation on grounds of "military need," the authorities exploited laws and regulations enabling them to carry out a program of compulsory purchase and seizure of private property. In East Jerusalem, which was formally annexed in 1967, the relevant laws allowed the government to lease parts of the 20,000 dunams thus seized (one-third of the total area annexed) to private Israeli individuals, who built vast housing estates comprising more than 30,000 apartments. In the West Bank, the operative laws remained Jordanian, and therefore the properties thus seized could not be used directly for the construction of settlements. Instead, they were earmarked for the public use of settlers (to build roads, cesspools, boreholes, water reservoirs, transmitters, sewage and water lines, firing ranges, and parking lots). Even so, in the early 1970s, 32,000 dunams of land in this category were allocated for the Ma'aleh-Adumim settlement and industrial construction.

Finally, the government proceeded to identify and seize "public land." Following a special Israeli cabinet

decision in 1980, public land was defined as all unreg-
istered and uncultivated land and retermed "state land."
In addition to previously registered government property, public land thus defined amounted to 2,150,000
dunams—i.e., about 39 percent of the total area of the
West Bank (5,500,000 dunams). State land is supervised
by the Custodian of Government and Abandoned Property, who routinely signs contracts transferring government lands to the World Zionist Organization (for the
establishment of Israeli settlements), to the Ministry of
Housing (for the establishment of construction sites in
townships), and to individual building contractors on
lease agreements.

A total of 2,268,500 dunams—41 percent of the West
Bank—fall into the categories of state land, requisitions,
closure, and compulsory purchase, and are under direct
Israeli control. In addition to this area, however, the
Israeli authorities have effectively "neutralized" a further 570,000 dunams by declaring them out of bounds
for Palestinian urban development. The total area subject to Israeli seizure or restrictions therefore amounts
to 2,838,500 dunams, or 52 percent of the area of the
West Bank. In the Gaza District, sixteen Jewish settlements have been established through similar processes.

During the first ten years of occupation, under Labor
governments, twenty-four settlements were established
in the West Bank. Settlement patterns reflected the
strategy of the Allon Plan (with the main emphasis being
on the Jordan Valley and Gush Etzion). Since then,
approximately 118 more settlements have been built,
distributed throughout the area in such a way as to
prevent any future Israeli withdrawal from the West

Bank and Gaza. In the West Bank, the settlements are distributed in several different clusters or groups, but the 1986 West Bank Data Project report shows that the bulk of settler concentration is limited to 18 percent of the West Bank land, with the heavily populated urban settlements being in the metropolitan areas of Jerusalem and Tel Aviv, along the Green Line. However, this very area happens to be where 40 percent of the total Palestinian West Bank population is concentrated.

Meanwhile, the number of settlers has shot up rapidly since 1980, reflecting the "Hundred Thousand Settler Plan," which envisaged increasing the number of settlers in the West Bank and Gaza by close to 80,000 (from a figure of about 25,000). According to the settlers' magazine *Nikuda*, by autumn 1986 the plan had achieved 65 percent success in terms of numbers of settlers and 80 percent success in terms of numbers of settlement points. The heaviest population concentrations, according to the West Bank Data Project report, are in urban as opposed to rural settlements, in the Jerusalem environs, the Tulkarm subdistrict, and Kiryat Arba.

A quick survey of the internal development within the settlements, and especially within the six major urban settlements or "towns," reveals that in addition to the strong ideology motivating the settlers, a major drive is under way to link these settlements institutionally and economically to the Israeli system. As an example, Ariel (inhabited now by approximately 8,000 settlers, but planned to absorb 100,000 inhabitants on an area totaling 30,000 dunams) already contains governmental offices of various ministries (communications, trade and industry, labor and social welfare, housing and construction, transport) together with the local police station and court of law. It already has at least nineteen major manufacturers/businesses, with an additional five under construction. Also under construction in Ariel is the Samaria College (for science, technology, administration, and rehabilitation), which will have an association with a campus in Kedumin, another urban settlement farther north. For purposes of degree accreditation, the Samaria College will be incorporated into Bar-Ilan University.

What Is to Be Done?

Many of the settlers are motivated by a strong sense of mission, which resonates throughout Israeli society. They believe that in resettling Judaea and Samaria, the heartland of the ancient Jewish commonwealth, they are fulfilling a religious or historical injunction to redeem the Jewish patrimony. Some are even convinced that the settlement of the land is a necessary prelude to the coming of the Messiah. These people are essentially dedicated to an ideological vision of Jewish reconstruction in the land of their biblical forefathers. They are not moved by the instrumental logic of personal lifestyle, which attracts other settlers, or of national security, which prompts many in the Israeli body politic to sympathize with the settlement movement, although they are perfectly willing to emphasize these themes in order to cultivate wider support. These settlers feel a quasi-mystical relationship with the land that requires possession, rather than mere presence. This attitude indicates that maintaining their present status would therefore be incompatible with peace based on an independent Palestinian state in the West Bank and Gaza. Not only are these settlers likely to put up a strong—perhaps even violent—preliminary opposition to a peace treaty between the Israeli government and the Palestinians, but they will continue to pose a destabilizing factor in the aftermath of an agreement that perpetuates their current political-legal status. There is therefore no room for extraterritoriality or extended sovereignty for Israeli settlements within a Palestinian state.

In theory, the removal of Jewish settlers would probably enhance the ultimate stability of Israeli-Palestinian relations in the long term. However, the extent of Jewish settlement in the West Bank and Gaza, the vested interests involved, the general sympathy within Israeli society for the settlers (at least in the abstract), and the traumatic memory of the evacuation of the Yamit settlement in Sinai in 1982, mean that the forcible evacuation of these settlers is simply inconceivable. No Israeli government would be willing or able to carry out such a measure, and there is therefore no alternative but to formulate some arrangement that combines incentives for voluntary "repatriation" to Israel and continued residence of Jews in their present homes in a manner consistent with both the principle of Palestinian sovereignty and the interests of individual Palestinians whose private property has been expropriated since 1967.

Incentives in the form of financial assistance, valid for a limited period of time, would presumably encourage many to relocate to Israel; many of the settlers now living in the occupied territories are motivated less by ideology than by pragmatic considerations. They do not see themselves as being in competition with the Palestinians for control of the land, and in fact would probably have preferred to live within the Green Line had suitable housing been available for them. Their decision to move to the West Bank was facilitated by the sense that they were still living in Israel. Once this changes, remaining there will be much less attractive; few would be enamored by the idea of living under Palestinian rule, and the departure of those who choose not to stay will make available infrastructural assets to the Palestinian state. On the other hand, some individuals may prefer, for a variety of reasons, to stay where they are, regardless of the political disposition of the territories, on condition that they could continue to enjoy quick and easy access to their places of work within the Green Line. Theoretically, and in the context of a suitable model of open borders, such individuals can remain in their current homes. But they will do so as individuals rather than as parts of collective communities structurally linked to the Israeli system.

In *The Geopolitics of Israel's Border Question*, Saul Cohen proposes the establishment of a "millet" system in which centers of Jewish residence can be offered full communal autonomy, exempting their subjects from local jurisdiction. Such residents will have rights of permanent residence, but will continue enjoying their Israeli citizenship. The author goes on to suggest that a quid pro quo arrangement may be reached whereby expatriate Arabs may be allowed to reside in villages in the Little Triangle or in the small Arab cores of such urban centers as Ramle, Haifa, and Jaffa, in exchange for the large Jewish exurban expansion from the Tel Aviv region to "such desirable Samarian mountain areas as Ariel . . ."

While there may be an imbalance in the basic nature of the comparison involved (as Palestinian residents and populated centers within Israel, regardless of the limited municipal autonomy involved, continue to be subject to Israeli jurisdiction), it is nevertheless possible to imagine a situation in which Jewish communities (as opposed to individuals) can indeed have a measure of municipal autonomy, similar to the status of Arab municipalities in Israel, which still falls under the overall jurisdiction of the central state authority. It may even be possible to have arrangements whereby the Israeli government is authorized by the relevant Palestinian authorities to subsidize services or construction required by that community, just as various Arab benefactors may be able to provide financial assistance to Arab communities in Israel. The very concept of balancing such possibilities against allowing "coastal" Palestinian expatriates to be rehabilitated in certain localities within the Green Line is refreshingly imaginative; aside from encouraging a tolerable reformulation of existing facts, it also addresses the important psychological component underlying the "refugee problem."

In addition to such individuals or communities, one must also provide for settlements or estates which were legitimately purchased by Jewish owners, either before 1948 or since 1967. Jews who continue to hold their Israeli citizenship would be accorded permanent residence rights in accordance with Palestinian laws. Should any group (e.g., Neturei Karta) or individual wish to apply for Palestinian citizenship, there should be nothing in the law to prevent this, and nothing to prevent an Israeli Jew from living and acquiring property in a Palestinian state. But as in the case of any other sovereign authority, the future Palestinian Home Office or Interior Ministry must not be constrained in advance concerning whatever regulations and arrangements that must be met for residence eligibility. Such rules may deal with the number of individuals who may apply in any one year, or with the amount or type of property that may be purchased by foreign nationals. But under all circumstances, any foreign national resident in the country must abide by its laws and be subject to its authority, as is the case in any sovereign state.

5

Water

Conflict over control of water sources has been a permanent feature in the history of the Middle East, as of most other semiarid regions in the world. In recent times, exploitation of the Euphrates River has complicated relations among Iraq, Syria, and Turkey. Egypt's abiding interest in Sudanese and Ethiopian affairs is explained by the fact that its lifeline, the Nile River, passes through those two countries. The Yarmuk River has at times been a contentious issue in Syrian-Jordanian relations, and Arabs have often suspected Israel of coveting control of the Litani River in Lebanon. The development of Israel's National Water Carrier and Syrian attempts to divert headwaters of the Jordan River played a part in the chain of events leading to the Arab-Israeli war of 1967. For a region of rapidly growing population, depletion of existing sources, and unpredictable repletion rates, water is not only an economic resource; it has existential value.

Geography and economic needs suggest that water

will be a central issue in Israeli-Palestinian relations and a major point of contention in negotiations on a political resolution of the conflict. The most salient geographical fact is that some of the large aquifers—the major underground water resources west of the Jordan— straddle the line separating Israel from the West Bank. Israeli agriculture, especially in the densely populated coastal plain, is highly dependent on these aquifers and would be adversely affected if a local authority in the West Bank were to develop a modern system of wells and pumping equipment at the highest catchments without due regard for Israeli needs. So frightening was the specter of future water diversion that in the mid-1970s a Labor government generally opposed to Jewish settlement in the West Bank nevertheless decided to establish a small number of settlements in Samaria, a few kilometers east of the Green Line, in order to forestall the possibility that the initial catchments of the western aquifer would be turned over to foreign control.

At the same time, Palestinians view these subterranean sources as primarily West Bank aquifers, partly because of their location and partly because they are fed by rains falling on the central mountain ridge. The Palestinians obviously hope that more water from these reservoirs will be available for agricultural and industrial development and population growth following independence than has been the case since 1967, given Israeli restrictions on drilling permits and water allocations to Palestinians. All of this indicates that a mutually acceptable agreement on water usage will be difficult to achieve, especially in the absence of comprehensive, region-wide water-sharing schemes. However, there is room for some optimism.

Total renewable subterranean aquifers wholly or

partly in the West Bank can provide approximately 615 million cubic meters (MCM) per annum. At the present time, Israeli wells within the Green Line draw about 300–350 MCM from these aquifers, almost 15 percent of Israel's total annual consumption of 1,900 MCM. The 27 artesian wells drilled by Israel since 1967 in the West Bank, mostly in the Jordan Valley for the use of Israeli settlements, account for another 20 MCM. By contrast, 382 artesian wells provide West Bank Palestinians with about 50 MCM from groundwater reserves, approximately one-third of their total annual consumption for agricultural, industrial, and household uses (the remainder comes from the 295 springs in the area, seep-surface water, and the cisterns with which many houses are equipped). In other words, the overall water balance for the area as a whole remains positive, by as much as 200 MCM.

After Palestinian independence, unexploited reserves together with water now used by Israeli settlers (much of which would presumably be available to Palestinian authorities) would make possible a significant increase in Palestinian usage before an overall water shortage developed. Moreover, there are substantial potential resources which are currently not used at all.

It is estimated that the average total annual rainfall in the West Bank is approximately 2,900 MCM. Even with a high rate of evapotranspiration (2,000 MCM) and runoff (64 MCM), the West Bank is still left with an overall water balance of 836 MCM, which is far in excess of present utilization rates by Palestinians, and still in excess of present utilization rates of West Bank waters by Palestinians and Israelis combined. Much of this potential excess can be exploited by a capital-intensive program to improve the capture, storage, distribution, and utilization of water. For example, the introduction of certain irrigation techniques (such as the more extensive use of drip systems) or even just a more efficient system of tapping the annual rainfall (through the use of reservoirs and the artificial recharge of shallow aquifers) would produce a much more promising hydrological picture for the West Bank; an American-funded project for recharging Gaza aquifers is already under way. And even within the present hydrological parameters, it is possible to improve water utilization for domestic use and agricultural/industrial expansion. Not only could rates of production in currently irrigated agricultural areas (about 77,000 dunams) be increased; such areas could be expanded. Moreover, new tracts of hitherto untouched lands, especially synclinal tracts on the eastern slopes of the West Bank hills, could be developed.

In short, a Palestinian state can potentially have far more water resources at its disposal than are currently available to Palestinians in the West Bank, even without curtailing the use that Israel makes of shared aquifers for agriculture within the Green Line. However, in the West Bank context, as indeed in the larger regional context, mutual understanding must be reached to prevent harmful and wasteful exploitation of water resources. In particular, it will be necessary to conclude an agreement on noninterference with the flow of underground water, particularly to the western Samaria aquifer, whose water table is already low. Because of the angle of inclination toward the coastal plain, there is a danger of seepage from the Mediterranean. Although some experts estimate that additional use can be made of the Turonian, Upper Cenomanian, and Lower Cenomanian aquifers, unregulated pumping in this area would result in excessive salination and contamination of a water source vital to the coastal plain of Israel.

The water situation in Gaza is much worse. Because of high salinity, many of the wells there are already useless for agriculture, and rapid population growth means that the water supply may soon become inadequate even for household needs. Indeed, some experts claim that this is already happening.

Palestinians can therefore be expected to insist that any water agreement with Israel be such as to guarantee Gaza's future needs. At one stage President Sadat toyed with the idea of directing water from the Nile to Israel's Negev desert. Various tentative studies were made by experts to show how this might be possible as well as cost-effective. The scenarios included one that envisaged the exploitation of the right angles of inclination to transfer water inside pipelines. Although recent projections of domestic Egyptian needs may make such ideas impractical, it is nevertheless worthwhile to bear them in mind during the course of negotiations, given their potential benefit both to regions in the Negev and to the Gaza District of the Palestinian state.

Yet another approach to the water problem in Gaza is to consider an agreement with Israel according to which the Gaza District may benefit, alongside regions in the Negev, from Israel's National Water Carrier. The National Water Carrier is Israel's major water project, and it consists of a network of pipes, open canals, and boosters which enables all regions in the country, including the Negev, to benefit from Israel's major natural reservoir: Lake Kinneret or Tiberias. This lake, which is almost 165 square kilometers in area, can hold up to 3 billion cubic meters of water. Apart from direct rainfall, the lake is fed by the Jordan River, which is itself fed by three sources, the Hasbani spring in Lebanon, the Banias spring on the Golan Heights (still claimed by Syria), and the Dan in northern Israel.

This last fact alone is enough to explain why water projects along the Jordan and close to its source have historically been a point of friction. Furthermore, one of the Jordan's tributaries (the Yarmuk River) forms part of the Syrian-Jordanian border, and Jordan itself draws very heavily on the waters of the river for its expanding agricultural projects along the eastern flank of the valley. As a result, water projects by any of the riparian states have almost invariably led to tension with other regional actors. A unilateral action on the part of Syria to divert the river close to its source would deprive Israel of a virtual lifeline. Indeed, unilateral actions by any of the parties contiguous to that area are bound to affect adversely the interests of the other parties in that area. Yet it stands to reason that the waters should be shared by the countries in which or along whose borders the Jordan River runs. In addition to Jordan, Syria, and Israel, another country which would fall into this category would be the new Palestinian state. It is conceivable that the primary benefits that this state will derive from the river waters will be indirect, for example, through an agreement with Israel to make use of its National Water Carrier or to purchase at reduced rates certain water-intensive agricultural produce from Israel.

The main point to be stressed is that future population growth and economic development require a more comprehensive, regional approach to the water problem. Lebanon, for example, has an abundance of water that exceeds the country's own needs; much of the

Litani's huge flow simply runs into the sea. Further afield, Turkey and Iraq have large water surpluses, which could be made available on a commercial basis; if Syria's and Jordan's needs were assured from such sources, for example, they might be far less dependent on access to water sources in the Lebanese-Israeli-Palestinian complex. Political obstacles—domestic instabilities and international conflicts—have prevented the effective exploitation of regional resources, including regional sharing schemes. Within the context of a political settlement of the Israeli-Arab conflict, it should be possible to remove many of these obstacles and secure an important economic advantage for all parties.

6

Jerusalem

Many observers believe that Jerusalem will prove to be the most difficult issue to be addressed in negotiations. Even those on both sides otherwise disposed toward reconciliation and compromise are likely to adopt a rigid, if not completely inflexible, position on Jerusalem. Indeed, Jerusalem is so contentious an issue that there seems to be something in the very nature of the problem that renders it irresolvable. It is possible, however, that Jerusalem is primarily a symbolic lodestone, on which all the emotions and sentiments of the conflict are focused. Whether Jerusalem's intractability is due to something inherent or symbolic is of enormous significance. If an issue is irresolvable due to its very nature, then nothing more can be said about it. If, on the other hand, its apparent intractability is a function of its symbolic role—of the fact that it embodies the fullest articulation of the emotions and prejudices people have toward the sum of issues comprising the entire conflict— then a way may be found to defuse those issues one by one so that the conflict as a whole begins to assume a tractable shape, and Jerusalem can then also be approached like other issues which lend themselves to a rational solution.

In the context of the present-day conflict between Israel and the Palestinians, there are certain features that bear on the Jerusalem issue. The first of these is the 1949 Armistice line (the so-called Green Line), which divided Israel and the West Bank until June 1967. This line also divided Jerusalem into two parts: East and West. This was not a line based on patterns of Arab and Jewish residence or property holding; before 1949, Jews lived in the eastern part and they still own property there, while Arabs lived in the western part and still own property there. However, between 1949 and 1967 this line divided Jerusalem into an Arab and an Israeli "part." Obviously, there is nothing intrinsically sacrosanct about the 1949 armistice line, either in Jerusalem or in the rest of the country. It can, however, provide some kind of tentative guideline for drawing boundaries for certain purposes, although such boundaries will necessarily be porous, since properties (including, for example, cemeteries) of the two communities will straddle the line wherever it is drawn.

The second feature to be borne in mind is Israel's unilateral act of annexation of the eastern part of the city through a Knesset law passed in 1967 which reflected the distinction made in Israeli psychology, and henceforth in Israeli law, between East Jerusalem and the rest of the West Bank. This distinction meant that Israel was able to carry out far more fundamental changes to the status quo in East Jerusalem than in the rest of the territories that came under its control in June 1967, although a by-product has been that East

Jerusalem Arabs were entitled to certain advantages denied residents of the West Bank. Among those changes has been the expansion of the municipal boundary of the city at the expense of West Bank territory. Unlike the expansion proposed, but never implemented, by the Jordanian government in May 1967, the Israeli expansion meticulously avoids most of the main surrounding Arab neighborhoods—Beit Hanina, Bir Nabala, al-Ram, Hizma, Anata, El-Ezariyya, and Abu Dis. On the other hand, there has been an intensive effort to construct Jewish neighborhoods within the new municipal boundary—Ramot, Ramat Eshkol, Atarot, Neve Ya'akov, Neve Ya'akov South, Giv'at Shapira, East Talpiot, and Gilo—and to rehabilitate the Jewish Quarter in the Old City. It is estimated that close to 120,000 Jewish residents now live in those neighborhoods, which is almost equal to the number of the Arabs within the expanded municipal boundary on the eastern side of the Green Line. During the same period, the Arab population has also grown substantially—more than doubled since 1967—but restrictions on building permits have led to severe housing shortages.

Third, whereas Israel lays claim to the entire city (within its enlarged municipal borders) and has declared it its eternal capital, Palestinians who seek a settlement generally regard only East Jerusalem as the capital of their Palestinian state. Nevertheless, a resolution of the Jerusalem issue, even more than of other "visible" components of the conflict, must be predicated on a very advanced form of unification or integration. The Israeli consensus in favor of a united city is virtually complete, and many Palestinian leaders who advocate that East Jerusalem be the capital of the Palestinian state have also been known to advocate the existence of a "united city." In other words, very few people, whatever their political persuasion, would wish to see the city redivided by a physical wall. This preference stems partly from the perception that there is something unnatural about a divided city. In this sense, a city is not undifferentiated matter which can be easily disaggregated. Instead, it resembles an integrated entity like a joint-stock company or a water system, whose division produces less than the sum of its parts, or even a living organism, whose division results in death. Thus, the Berlin Wall always seemed more of a distortion than the border dividing the two Germanys, or the two Koreas. A physical border dividing East from West Jerusalem would also seem much more of a distortion than any border line dividing Israel from Palestine, and the challenge is therefore to determine whether there is some formula for shared ownership and/or participation that can ensure the integrity of the city while satisfying the political and emotional requirements of both sides.

There are no specific proposals or schemata published or offered by Palestinians that address this need. Palestinians have ordinarily just declared their preference for reestablishing the Armistice line, although some have admitted the need to keep the border open. On the other hand, several Israeli authors and politicians have tried to provide general sketches or outlines of proposed solutions to the problem of Jerusalem.

One of the co-authors of this work has already argued in his book *A Palestinian State: The Implications for Israel* that the apparent irreconcilability of views concerning Jerusalem can be overcome, if at all, only by deliberately "obfuscating" the issue of sovereignty. While Jerusalem would remain physically united under overall Israeli control, it could, through a variety of measures, be made to seem sufficiently bipolitical through the following special arrangements: first, that it be delineated through gateways at the municipal borders from both the Israeli and Palestinian territories (for any immigration, customs, or security procedures applying to movement between the two states); second, that its united municipal government (headed by its elected Israeli mayor and Arab deputy mayor) assume wide functions, including some of those that are normally borne by the state government (e.g., its own policing units, postal services and stamps, vehicle licensing); third, that neighborhood councils or boroughs corresponding to religioethnic residence patterns be granted functional authority to supervise facilities such as education and other main support services; and fourth, that religious properties and interests be removed from the formal jurisdiction of any national authority and be placed under the supervision of the municipal government, with the clear intention of retaining the present system of self-administration by the different religious authorities.

The "obfuscation" of the sovereignty issue can be interpreted as an attempt to address the problem functionally and to achieve a measure of "divisibility" through a devolution of authority. In the same spirit, the longtime mayor of Jerusalem, Teddy Kollek, has argued, in his 1988 *Foreign Affairs* article, that "after 21 years of administering Jerusalem as one city, we know that all communities, but in particular the Arab one, need a much larger measure of self-administration, autonomy or functional sovereignty." In his view, "the municipality needs much more of the authority now vested in the government of Israel so that it can share this local authority with the communities and neighborhoods." Kollek further states that "the future of Jerusalem is to remain united and the capital of Israel, under the overall sovereignty of Israel. There is, however, room for functional division of authority, for internal autonomy of each community and for functional sovereignty."

In terms of substance, the distinction made here between "functional sovereignty" and "sovereignty" is one of degree rather than of kind. In some ways, it resembles the ultimate difference between "autonomy in the West Bank" and "state in the West Bank." After all, many Israelis who are against the establishment of (even a demilitarized) Palestinian state are nevertheless prepared to support "super-autonomy" for the Palestinians and are willing to assign to an autonomous entity almost the same measure of authority which the proponents of the state idea would be prepared to allocate to a Palestinian state.

Moshe Amirav, a former Likud central committee member and then a Shinui councillor in Kollek's municipality, approaches the issue somewhat differently. In early 1990, he proposed that Israel waive sovereignty "over part of the city." But first, he argued, the city boundary should again be extended (doubled so as to cover some 500 square kilometers) along the east-west and north-south axes. The Israeli axis, running east-west, would include Ma'aleh Adumim at the easternmost point and Mevasseret Zion in the west. The Palestinian axis, running north-south, would include Ramallah in the north and Bethlehem in the south. Altogether, Amirav's borders are closer to the municipal boundaries proposed by the United Nations in 1947 than to today's extended borders. Amirav suggested that the Israeli sovereign axis include "the Jewish part" of Jerusalem, while the Palestinian sovereign axis include "the Arab part of Jerusalem." The Jerusalem metropolitan area could be declared a free-trade area, and there could be a Jewish municipality as well as an Arab municipality with a joint roof council for the entire metropolis. The chairmanship of the metropolitan municipality would rotate between Jew and Arab. In conclusion, therefore, Amirav proposed that there be an open city, a united metropolis, a dual sovereignty, with two capitals.

Once again, the Amirav proposal seems to address the "obfuscation" issue, but from a different angle. While a division of sovereignty is envisioned in nominal terms, in practice this division almost melts as soon as functional authorities begin to be divided up. The approach of one of these co-authors (in the previously cited work) is the exact opposite: a sufficient measure of devolution of authority is envisioned, almost reaching the point where the unilateral assertion of all-encompassing Israeli sovereignty begins to assume a merely nominal shape at its Arab limit.

What is now needed is a combination of clarity and obfuscation at different levels, which would simultaneously satisfy both the aspiration for distinctiveness/ independence and the imperative of integration and unification. The precise formula must be politically creative and technically complex, and what follows is simply an attempt to lay out its underlying principles and basic guidelines. A more detailed blueprint could emerge only after lengthy negotiations.

The aspiration for distinctiveness/independence implies that the Palestinian state as well as Israel has a distinct title to different parts of the city. Border lines can demarcate these titles by defining the boundaries of Jewish and Arab neighborhoods, which Palestinians would wish to regard as sovereignty lines and Israelis as limits of jurisdictional responsibility for two local councils. In general, these lines will distinguish between the main Jewish and Arab population clusters, but they can also delineate other areas, such as Sharafat and Beit Safafa in the predominantly Jewish region of the city and Neve Ya'acov and Giv'at Shapira in the predominantly Arab part. These lines can also help to specify the communal standing of properties, burial grounds, or building complexes which happen (or have been consciously planned) to fall across intercommunal boundaries. Because of the scattered disposition of the various regions and clusters, these lines will frequently intersect.

At the same time, boundary lines will not in any way undermine the continued physical and functional unity of the city. In practical terms, they will simply specify the municipal limits of the two sets of Jewish and Arab neighborhoods. But instead of breaking up each set of such neighborhoods (and in particular the Arab set) to the point of obliterating any sense of national or cultural unity through a system of "neighborhood councils," this arrangement will address the collective psychological need for some form of higher-level government, through the establishment of separate municipal councils for each set of neighborhoods.

Thus, Israel's Jerusalem and Palestine's Jerusalem will each have a separate municipal council that will govern intercrossing and intersecting neighborhoods and areas which are divided by imaginary sovereign lines. Israel's Jerusalem will be its capital, while Palestine's Jerusalem will be its capital, housing the seat of its government. Residents will be able to express their separate sense of identity through the culture-specific activities of their council: school curricula and language of instruction, recreational and cultural affairs, celebration of holidays, and certain other functions such as the distribution of some types of licenses and permits. For the most part, the daily lives of residents will proceed along well-established patterns. Religious affairs and matters of personal status (marriage, divorce, inheritance, etc.) will continue to be regulated by the millet system of self-governing communal authorities established in Ottoman times. In civil and criminal matters not covered by municipal ordinances, Jews and Arabs will ordinarily be subject to Israeli and Palestinian law, respectively. However, legal disputes, claims, or criminal cases may arise involving members of different communities in Jerusalem, and since there may be some inconsistencies between the Israeli and Palestinian legal systems, a metropolitan code of laws should be enacted to deal with such cases. The activities of the two municipal councils can be financed by some proportion of property taxes, grants-in-aid by respective national governments, and private contributions.

The second imperative—for integration and unification—can be satisfied by a metropolitan or roof municipality elected by all residents of Jerusalem. The political structure should be based on neighborhoods or wards which would send representatives to the metropolitan government. The objective of the electoral system should be to encourage binational coalitions, and in any event to ensure that the demographic imbalance in the metropolis does not reflect itself in discriminatory measures or planning policies. The metropolitan government should supervise common, relatively emotion-free issues such as water and sewage, roads and urban transportation, firefighting, sanitation, and traffic and tourist departments, and it should be administratively responsible for the Jerusalem police force. Its legal department, perhaps composed of individuals seconded from the Israeli and Palestinian Justice Ministries, can draft the special Jerusalem code mentioned above to regulate intercommunal traffic, commercial, or even criminal cases where Israeli law and Palestinian law diverge, and a municipal court system can rule on cases covered by the code. Another issue that can be regulated by the metropolitan government is zoning, especially insofar as it refers to demographic development. This is obviously an area where unilateral acts would be destabilizing, and joint control would minimize conflict and provide the mechanism for reaching rational solutions.

The noncoercive character of life in the city can also be enhanced by establishing the use of both Israeli and Palestinian currency in Jerusalem and permitting residents or visitors, whenever there are parallel mechanisms available (e.g., postage stamps), to choose freely between them.

The metropolis can be allocated a special status by the two states, endowing it with some governmental functions (e.g., collection of licensing and postal fees) that will enable it to institute high-level coordination on various matters of city concern and to raise funds beyond local property taxes which may be necessary to finance municipal activities. The metropolis itself will have a delineated (continuous) border line, and this border line may be used for any number of purposes to the benefit of the city, such as its being declared a free-trade zone, in which case its main entrances/exits can be used for purposes of customs and security control. Of course, they will also resemble border-crossing points, but their actual operation will be a function of the "porous" border line separating the two states (see Chapter 2, "The Demarcation and Meaning of Borders").

In essence, such an arrangement in Jerusalem will simultaneously protect the rights of its inhabitants while providing for maximal integration. What in fact was impossible to achieve since 1967, when the physical barriers went down, will become a tangible reality once the "reengagement" between the two parts of the city is adjusted to take Palestinian aspirations into account. Recent research shows that according to accepted indicators the city is currently more divided than many other problematic binational cities. Indeed, Jerusalem is less integrated than it was before 1948, when the city was binational under British rule, and since 1987 social segregation has increased even more as a result of the intifada.

Conflict and imbalance have prevented Jerusalem from playing a unifying role between religious and cultural groups that might be possible under more settled circumstances. Not only could Jerusalem be the natural seat of joint financial institutions and businesses; it might also provide a venue for joint religious and cultural study centers and academies. A judicious combination of integration and separation in Jerusalem can work to the benefit of both sides and of the city itself.

7

Regionalization and Internationalization

The Middle East Regional Dimension of a Two-State Settlement

The Israeli-Arab conflict does not involve Israelis and Palestinians alone. Israel is formally in a state of war with most Arab states. Historically, this situation stems from Arab solidarity with the Palestinians, but there are many other issues that impinge on Israeli-Arab relations. Israel and Syria are parties to a dispute over the disposition of the Golan Heights, which was conquered by Israel in 1967 and effectively annexed in 1981; Israel, Syria, Jordan, and Lebanon have found themselves in competition for scarce water resources, and this competition may well intensify in the future; Israel and several Arab states (especially Iraq) are locked into destabilizing arms races; and Israel has reserved claims against Arab states for abandoned Jewish property.

Moreover, many provisions of an Israeli-Palestinian settlement cannot be implemented without the political endorsement and practical support of Arab states. Normalization of relations with Israel and region-wide arms-control and confidence-building measures are also needed to relieve Israeli concerns about the risks inherent in territorial concessions. In short, no resolution of the Israeli-Arab conflict can be definitive and durable unless it is a comprehensive, regional agreement, and this requires the settlement of outstanding differences between Israel and Arab states as well as material support by Arab states to implement the Israeli-Palestinian agreement.

Political Matters

In principle, Arab endorsement of an Israeli-Palestinian peace settlement should not be difficult to secure. By designating the PLO as the sole legitimate spokesman of the Palestinians, all the Arab states have implicitly signaled their disinterest in the substance of an Israeli-Palestinian settlement and some have explicitly stated that they will approve any terms acceptable to the PLO. However, at least three factors complicate this seemingly straightforward situation.

The first concerns radical states which may reject the envisaged Israeli-Palestinian settlement because they object either to its specific terms or to the very principle of peace with Israel. These objections may be simple posturing, perhaps in the hope of improving some regime's domestic and/or regional standing, or they may stem from ideological conviction of the type expressed by fundamentalist or ultranationalist movements. In either case, they raise the prospect of some regional factors being "more Catholic than the Pope." Rejectionism of this sort would complicate the viability of a peace settlement, but it would not be a debilitating obstacle unless it emanated from a state able to exert a strong influence on the policy of a Palestinian state otherwise committed to peace or to pose a substantial military threat to Israel. In other words, it would depend on the source of the rejectionism. If, for example, there were a general Arab consensus in favor of the settlement and subversive challenges emanated only from Libya or (if inspired by Islamic fervor) Iran, the structure of peace would be strong enough to withstand this threat. If, on the other hand, a state like Syria or Iraq were actively to oppose the settlement—by means of hostile propaganda, encouragement of dissident Palestinian groups, or the promotion of military tensions with Israel—the chances are that an Israeli-Palestinian agreement would not be reached or that it would quickly fall apart. Therefore, the minimum requirement is that the Arab states close to the Israeli-Palestinian core, with large numbers of Palestinians or with important financial and/or military resources, also be incorporated into the settlement. In practice, this means the active, positive involvement of Syria, Jordan, Iraq, Saudi Arabia, and political forces in Lebanon, in addition to Egypt.

Arab endorsement of an Israeli-Palestinian settlement, at least at the declaratory level, may be far easier to achieve than many people believe. With the exception of Syria, these Arab countries accepted Security Council Resolution 242 of November 1967, which is predicated on the principle of peace with Israel. All of these countries, including Syria, accepted Security Council Resolution 338 of 1973, which calls for negotiations with Israel on the basis of Resolution 242. In 1982, Arab countries approved the "Fez peace plan," which calls for peace on the basis of Security Council Resolutions 242 and 338, in conjunction with the Palestinian right to set up an independent state. Following the

Palestine National Council (PNC) session in Algiers in November 1988, Arab countries reaffirmed their support of the Palestinian peace proposal and strategy for a lasting settlement with Israel. And during the Arab summit held in Baghdad in June 1990, all Arab countries in attendance (with the exception of Libya, which explicitly stated its reservations concerning the issue) reaffirmed their support of the Palestinian peace strategy adopted in November 1988. In other words, all Arab countries except Libya have implicitly endorsed the principle of peace with Israel as envisioned in the Palestinian strategy, and while they have not stated their own willingness to make peace in equally unambiguous terms, moving from implicit endorsement to explicit recognition should not be an insuperable problem.

However, beyond a principled willingness on the part of these states to make peace with Israel, their active involvement presupposes that outstanding bilateral problems will somehow be resolved and that the Arab states will ultimately make a positive contribution of their own to peaceful Israeli-Arab relations in the future. The most prominent bilateral problem is the disposition of the Golan Heights. Although it is difficult to envisage the precise character of a settlement of this issue, a restoration of the pre-1967 situation is as unacceptable to Israel as is the current status to Syria. Any negotiated agreement will therefore have to combine several elements, including the issue of demilitarization and other security arrangements. Beyond the territorial issue, there are potential conflicts over water rights which may destabilize Israel's future relations with Syria, Jordan, and Lebanon. The failure to address this problem, in the form of a comprehensive regional scheme for sharing and enhancing water resources, would mean leaving a time bomb ticking away that at some point might explode the entire structure of peace.

Circumstances require that Arab support for a peace settlement go beyond verbal endorsement of an Israeli-Palestinian agreement to include active ratification. The normalization of Palestinian national status and renunciation of further claims against Israel are major objectives of any agreement and conditions for its long-term viability. It is therefore vital that the "refugee problem" be eliminated as a political question. While other Arab states do not have direct responsibility for the resettlement of refugees in a Palestinian state and for any compensation agreements, their cooperation is nevertheless necessary if UNRWA camps in their own territory are to be disbanded and Palestinians there are to be offered the option of permanent residence (with or without local citizenship) and attendant legal rights (work permits, property ownership, etc.). Since it is unlikely that all the Palestinians now living in other Arab states would prefer to move to a Palestinian state (or that it could absorb them all if they did want to move), the "refugee problem" cannot be solved without the approval and support of Arab governments, and unless that approval and support are forthcoming, no definitive peace settlement is possible.

Financial and Economic Matters

While solidarity with the Palestinians and the political willingness to endorse a settlement with Israel would presumably facilitate Arab support for measures to entrench peace and stability in the Israeli-Arab arena, a truly durable settlement would require certain specific

Arab commitments in financial/economic and security matters. Insofar as finance and economics are concerned, Arab assistance to the Palestinian state would clearly be necessary to permit rehabilitation of the refugees already living in the West Bank and Gaza and the absorption of others who might arrive from elsewhere. Beyond the immediate infrastructure (housing, transportation, schools, electricity, sewage, etc.) and employment needs for this population, a more general development and reconstruction program would be needed to prevent political instabilities stemming from serious economic deprivation in the Palestinian state.

While actual financial needs cannot be defined without analyses and plans based on more precise information about population growth, it is clear that only part of the capital required could be generated by redirecting current assistance to Palestinians (UNRWA funds, subsidies to the PLO, etc.). Additional financing would undoubtedly come from a variety of other sources, including Western governments, foreign private investors, and the Palestinians themselves, but a major part of the burden would have to be borne by the Arab world, especially the oil-exporting states, and some kind of collective commitment, perhaps under the auspices of the Arab League, to underwrite a development fund should be an integral part of any settlement.

A two-state settlement will also entail major direct financial costs for Israel, including the relocation of some military facilities and compensation for Jewish settlers who choose not to remain in a Palestinian state. While precedents exist for financing the removal of foreign forces by the beneficiaries of that process—e.g., the German commitment to underwrite the costs of removing Soviet forces from East Germany—it would be unreasonable to make any Israeli withdrawal contingent on Arab funds earmarked for that purpose. On the other hand, it is entirely appropriate that peace include at least the potential opportunity for an overall improvement in Israel's economic condition. With respect to the Arab states, this means the abolition of the economic embargo and the institution of normal, nondiscriminatory trade practices vis-à-vis Israel.

The only specific financial obligation required from the Arab states is to pay compensation for abandoned and sequestered/nationalized Jewish property. Government persecution and hostile social environments, which accompanied the struggle to establish the Jewish state, compelled hundreds of thousands of Jews to leave Arab countries, usually without being able to remove or capitalize their property. The largest Jewish communities affected were in Iraq, Yemen, Egypt, and Morocco, but the phenomenon is common to every Arab country in which Jews once lived. There is no authoritative estimate of the value of the assets they left behind, but it is huge by any reckoning, and a comprehensive settlement of the conflict, involving compensation for Palestinian refugees, must also provide compensation for the material losses of Jews. While the procedures for compensation (direct payments to individuals or net lump-sum transfers to respective governments) may be worked out by the parties themselves, the actual value of assets should be calculated by an impartial body, such as the International Court of Justice or a special International Claims Commission set up for this purpose. Since the process of hearing and assessing claims will be long and arduous, it would be advisable to begin immediately so that provision can be made for the actual implementation of decisions during any transitional period called for in the settlement.

Security Matters

A comprehensive regional peace settlement requires comprehensive regional security arrangements. Without explicit measures to reduce military insecurities and enhance confidence, the peace settlement upon which normal political and economic relations are predicated will not be achieved. In particular, a settlement of the Israeli-Palestinian conflict will not improve Israeli security unless it also changes the threatening force postures of Arab states. A broad range of arms-control measures is potentially available to address this problem, some of them modeled on precedents from other areas (especially Europe), some of them specific to the Israeli-Arab context. Actions such as asymmetrical cuts in the disproportionately large military establishments of some Arab states and the restructuring of standing armies into defensively oriented reserve/militia forces would contribute greatly to regional military stability but might be difficult to incorporate into formal agreements. On the other hand, precisely focused measures such as acceptance of demilitarized or limited-forces zones similar to those established by the Israeli-Egyptian peace treaty and a ban on the introduction of foreign forces into Jordan should be incorporated into peace treaties. To reduce the risks of miscalculation and unintended confrontations, provisions should also be made for prior notification of tests and maneuvers, exchanges of military observer missions, and direct military-to-military communication. There are particular complexities associated with weapons of mass destruction because of uncertainties in the verification of bans or limitations, because of linkages among different categories of such weapons, and especially because of the relationship between these weapons and the overall conventional military balance. As a matter of general principle, these weapons should be limited or eliminated, provided credible verification is possible, but this goal is attainable, if at all, only within the context of a general security regime that provides safeguards for Israel against the intrinsic conventional military potential of Arab demographic and economic resources.

Procedural Considerations

Although it is widely assumed that an Israeli-Palestinian settlement must somehow be linked to a broader Israeli-Arab settlement, there is far less consensus about the sequencing of these developments. Palestinians and many other Arabs insist that the Israeli-Palestinian dimension is the historical and substantive core of the conflict and that its resolution should be a prerequisite for peaceful relations between Israel and the rest of the Arab world. Israelis tend to believe that a settlement with the Palestinians involving territorial concessions is extremely imprudent, if not suicidal, unless the wider Arab rejection of Israel and the specific dangers of Arab belligerency are first eliminated.

Although the Arab states may well refuse to contract peace with Israel in the absence of an Israeli-Palestinian agreement, they are probably more concerned about the fact of such an agreement than about its specific terms. By the same token, the Arab states have not authorized the PLO to speak in their names—the Palestinians cannot "deliver" the Arabs—and there is no prior Arab consent to peace with Israel, much less to any particular requirements which Israel may have. As a result, the question of which comes first—the Palestinians or the Arab states—is misplaced. What are really needed are multiple bilateral negotiations between Israel and the Palestinians, and Israel and each of the relevant Arab states. Whether or not these take place in the same city and building or even begin at the same time is of secondary importance (although it may be instructive to note the precedent of the 1949 Armistice talks, in the course of which Israel negotiated simultaneously with several Arab states); the critical factor is the recognition that the different agreements are intrinsically interconnected and that their complete implementation is mutually contingent—i.e., that none of them can be fully carried out unless they are all fully carried out. It might, however, be possible to implement some transitional elements of an Israeli-Palestinian agreement pending the full implementation of the agreements with Arab states.

The Role of
Extraregional Powers

Unlike the Arab states, extraregional powers are not strictly essential to a resolution of the Israeli-Palestinian conflict. On the other hand, outside actors have important contributions to make, not as substitutes for an agreed settlement, but as facilitators of negotiations and providers of supplementary reassurance, in the form of political, economic, and military support to implement the settlement and improve the prospects for long-term stability in the region.

The first function involves classic mediation services: good offices, initial channels of communication, technical support, and good faith efforts to narrow seemingly irreconcilable differences or provide "side payments" to justify concessions that one or both of the parties would otherwise be unwilling to make. A mediator can only provide these services if he combines several qualities: a reputation for fairness and reliability, sufficient interest in a settlement to commit his own energies and resources in promoting the progress of negotiations, and sufficient disinterest in a settlement to refrain from attempting to become an arbitrator and impose terms rejected by one or both of the parties.

The second function involves reinforcement of agreements reached between the parties—i.e., additional monitoring and verification of provisions, credible guarantees of support for an aggrieved party in the event of a violation, and general assistance for economic and political stabilization. This function requires a third party to possess considerable economic, technological, and military resources of its own, a demonstrated willingness to use them, and the ability to mobilize additional resources from others. In the specific context of the Israeli-Palestinian and Israeli-Arab conflicts, the expectations from third parties include monitoring and observer forces, reassurance of support for Israeli and Palestinian or Arab defense needs in case the security arrangements in the peace agreements somehow break down, and assistance in financing the cost of any Israeli military and civilian redeployments, compensation for Palestinian refugees and Jewish property in Arab countries, and a Palestine economic development fund.

No single power has all the characteristics needed to fulfill either function. To the extent that any outside involvement is required to facilitate negotiations, the United States would appear to be the most logical candidate. However, Palestinian or other Arab suspicion due to America's historical association with Israel may cause them to prefer broader auspices, and the involvement of the Soviet Union as some kind of joint facilitator would therefore also be necessary.

Insofar as the second function is concerned—organizing post-settlement assistance—a major role can also be played by the European Community. After all, Euro-Israeli trade and Euro-Arab trade are already significant and can only be expected to increase in the post-1992 era. This means that a stable and vibrant economy in the Middle East will be of benefit to Europe. It will also be in the region's interest to align and adjust itself to the emerging economic reality nearby. Indeed, a concrete prospect of economic cooperation between the European Community and Israel/Palestine—which could possibly include Jordan, Lebanon, and Egypt as well—may be a further incentive to conclude a settlement. In any event, the institutionalized involvement of Europe and Japan in providing post-settlement assistance can only help consolidate the peace.

8

Implementation of the Agreement

Transition Arrangements

Phased implementation of an Israeli-Palestinian settlement is necessary for both political and practical reasons. Politically, it provides a mechanism and period of time for risk management and confidence building; during the transition period, the graduated transfer to Palestinians of authority and control over the territories to be evacuated by Israel can proceed in tandem with the demonstrated fulfillment of Palestinian and Arab commitments. On the practical level, phased implementation will be required to permit the orderly redeployment of Israeli personnel and facilities and the relocation of Jewish settlers who choose to move to Israel within its post-settlement borders, and to create or consolidate the constitutional order and the political and administrative institutions of the Palestinian state. Transition arrangements should therefore be an integral part of the peace agreement.

While it is impossible to describe in detail the entire process of building the Palestinian state, some of the most important features should be pointed out. Perhaps the most fundamental of these is the elaboration of a constitutional order. Almost immediately after a peace agreement is ratified by plebiscite (see below), Palestinians will have to define the structure and functions of their government: basic laws concerning government authority, individual rights and obligations, procedures for ordinary legislation and constitutional amendment, criteria for citizenship and selection of leadership, etc. Like most constitutional orders, this one will continue to evolve over time; like some, it may expire shortly after its promulgation or even be stillborn. Nevertheless, it is a logical point from which to begin the process.

While free elections for a constitutional convention would be the preferred method, the public will already be so involved in collective decision-making processes (a plebiscite on the peace treaty followed by elections for a government) that it would be more practical to assign the task of drafting a constitution to the Palestine National Council (PNC). For this purpose, the PNC could establish a special constitution commission which would be responsible for preparing a first draft, and it should be able to complete its work within six to nine months. The draft would then be submitted for the approval of the PNC, whose endorsement would lend it sufficient initial legitimacy. On the basis of this provisional constitution, general elections for national and local governments could then be held. In other words, these governments could be in place within eighteen to twenty-one months of the ratification of the peace agreement. The elections would simultaneously serve as a referendum on the constitution, and if an absolute majority of the voters (51 percent) opposed the constitution, the first task of the elected Assembly would be to propose necessary amendments.

To promote a more conducive atmosphere for ratification, it would be advisable for Israel to integrate senior Palestinian bureaucrats, more responsive to their own constituents, into the top levels of the civil administration as soon as the agreements are signed. It could also take other measures to reduce tensions. During the first phase after ratification, a Palestinian interim administration should be formally set up to begin working on the transfer of power and authority from Israeli to Palestinian hands. The simplest procedure would be to enlist the local national leadership—i.e., the representatives of various public and voluntary bodies (such as the Federation of Labor Unions, the Federation of Professional Unions, the Council for Higher Education, the Higher Women's Council, elected heads of municipalities and chambers of commerce, the Higher Health Council, the Higher Economic Council, and others). The main purpose of this administration would be to undertake elementary political and socioeconomic stabilization measures which the Israeli administration had previously been unable or unwilling to carry out (although there is nothing, in principle, to prevent Israeli initiatives on some of these measures while negotiations are going on, or even before they begin). More specifically, the interim administration's task would be twofold:

1. To normalize daily life by restoring the routine operations of government—school systems, tax collection, regular business hours, law enforcement (police and courts), etc.—which were disrupted at the beginning

of the intifada, and by dealing immediately with the most pressing hardships, such as release of administrative detainees, favorable review of requests for family reunification and travel permits; and

2. To lay the foundations for the economic development of the Palestinian state, by using taxes collected in the territories and funds from other sources to improve basic infrastructure (e.g., roads, sewage systems), by instituting a liberalized licensing policy (with respect to exports and imports, residential and factory construction, zoning of unused state lands) and a more equitable allocation of water resources, and by establishing a domestic banking system.

During this first phase, ultimate authority would still reside with the Israeli military government. However, the symbols of Palestinian statehood would come into immediate use, Palestinian civil servants would move into the highest ranks of the bureaucracy previously held by Israeli staff officers, and a variety of practices associated with the occupation regime (such as deportations, land expropriations, and building of new settlements or geographic expansion of existing ones) would be explicitly precluded by agreement.

After the election of regular national and municipal governments, the full and formal transfer of authority would take place. Palestinian ministers and senior civil servants would assume the responsibility for policy formulation and day-to-day administration in such areas as housing, agriculture, commerce and industry, education and culture, health, welfare, environment, labor, transportation, communications, taxation, immigration, foreign relations, justice, internal security and police, although they would continue to consult with Israeli liaison officers and advisers for purposes of transfer of files and information, technical assistance, and training of personnel. It is difficult to say precisely how long this phase would last, since it would depend on complex technical Israeli-Palestinian and Israeli-Arab arrangements (e.g., currency conversion, compensation to Palestinian refugees and Jews from Arab countries, etc.) and on the development of a whole range of Palestinian technical and administrative capabilities (e.g., establishing and managing such necessities as an airline, radio and television stations, telecommunications and postal networks), but also on the demonstrated fulfillment of treaty obligations (e.g., prevention of terrorism, the process of refugee rehabilitation in the Palestinian state and other Arab countries, development of trade and other peaceful relations between Israel and the Arab states). However, something in the range of five to seven years would appear to be appropriate.

At the beginning of this phase, the peace agreement would be formally incorporated into a treaty between the two states. Israeli military personnel would withdraw from Arab population centers in favor of Palestinian internal security forces and would either redeploy into Israel or move to other areas in the territories pending the completion of alternative facilities in Israel.

By the end of this phase, the only official Israeli personnel remaining in the Palestinian state would be observers and forces manning the military installations in the security zones specified in the agreement (see Chapter 1, "Security Arrangements"). These personnel would in no way impinge on the government of the Palestinian state and their continued presence could be reconsidered, perhaps five to ten years further on, in light of technological developments and overall political and strategic trends in the Middle East. As an integral part of the negotiated agreement, a joint review committee will be charged with the task of periodically reviewing the time schedules for the various phases.

Ratification

Any agreement, no matter how intrinsically "reasonable" or "fair" it may be, must be buttressed by measures to permit monitoring and verification of compliance with various obligations. To ensure that any violations are rectified before they become intolerably dangerous, there must also be guarantees of various sorts, including the possibility of self-help if all else fails. Such provisions are routinely made part of international agreements because the parties do not have unequivocal trust in the benign intentions of their adversaries or even in their ability to avoid unintended violations. Practical arrangements of this sort enhance confidence that the terms will be honored, and thereby enhance the chances that an agreement will be reached. Ultimately, however, any agreement must also be grounded in some presumption of good faith; there is simply no point in contracting an agreement if the working assumption is that the other side intends not to carry it out. The most important indicator of serious intent is widespread endorsement by the people in whose name an agreement is made.

Approval of a two-state settlement would be the most agonizing political decision ever made by either Israelis or Palestinians. Because of the gravity of the commitments and concessions involved, any agreement should be immunized, as much as possible, against subsequent accusations of betrayal. Immunization of this sort is difficult to achieve for several reasons. First of all, whatever the credentials of negotiators, they cannot authoritatively commit their own constituencies, particularly on a matter as weighty as this one. Second, the Palestinian side lacks representative institutions and constitutional procedures for contracting and ratifying international agreements. Third, there can be no absolute guarantee that approved agreements, though intended to be permanent, will actually be honored in perpetuity; there is no practical way to commit future generations.

All these considerations indicate that any agreement must include stringent requirements for ratification. The entire agreement, once negotiated, should therefore be made public and exposed to widespread debate and then be the subject of a plebiscite. Moreover, ratification should depend on something more than a simple majority—i.e., it should require approval by perhaps two-thirds of the respective populations. Without approval of this magnitude, it would be politically impossible for any Israeli government to fulfill the "land" part of the "land for peace" formula, and politically impossible for the Palestinians to achieve credibility for their commitment to the "peace" part.

In Israel, the mechanics of ratification should be fairly straightforward. Israel has a duly constituted government authorized to negotiate international agreements and a representative legislature which can approve or disapprove of government actions. Moreover, it is inconceivable that any government could implement an agreement such as this one without the approval of parliament (or, indeed, that it would not immediately be challenged in a motion of no confidence). In any

event, those parties favoring territorial compromise
have stated that they would put the question of concessions directly to the people. While a special election
might satisfy this requirement, the meaning of the
outcome could be obfuscated by other considerations
(personal popularity, support for parties based on social,
economic, ethnic, or religious grounds, etc.), and it
would therefore be preferable to hold a plebiscite in
which the single question would be "Do you approve
or disapprove of the proposed agreement?" The plebiscite could take place according to the rules governing
regular elections: qualified voters would be adult Israeli
citizens present in Israel or entitled to cast an absentee
ballot.

Circumstances make the process of Palestinian ratification more complicated. Until such time as there is a
Palestinian state, there will be no Palestinian government
to negotiate international agreements and no constitutional procedures for ratifying them or even for legally
defining the political community—i.e., the Palestinians
who are entitled to participate in these processes. On
the other hand, until there is a clearly defined method
for binding the Palestinians to a durable peace, even
Israelis otherwise prepared to agree to the establishment
of a Palestinian state will withhold their approval. The
only way to resolve this dilemma is to begin with the
Palestinian institutions that come closest to meeting
conventional criteria for a valid interlocutor and then
testing the popular willingness to endorse the package
of obligations and commitments on as wide a basis as
possible.

The counterparts that best approximate "normal"
political institutions are the PLO Executive Committee,
which has symbolic and some operational government

functions, and the Palestine National Council, which embodies various interests and constituencies and therefore resembles to some extent a legislature. In terms of their structure and composition, these institutions perforce suffer from constitutional defects; in particular, they do not effectively control any territory and their representative character has never been subjected to the test of elections, except in the case of some voluntary organizations (women, students, writers, etc.) whose electorates are self-selected. But whatever the defects of these institutions, no other Palestinian organizations publicly contest the legitimacy of their leading roles or appear to be viable alternatives. Consequently, the logical point of departure is with a negotiating delegation appointed or at least approved by the Executive Committee. Explicit Executive Committee approval of an agreement would be a necessary but not sufficient condition for ratification. In addition, the PNC would be required to endorse the agreement and to signal its intention to repeal the Palestine National Charter following popular approval of the agreement. Approval by the Palestinian public would be the only way to overcome the objections of individuals and organizations and of other Arab states and to establish the irreproachable legitimacy of the agreement—i.e., to protect it against subsequent accusations that it was a capitulationist document signed by unrepresentative politicians who had stabbed the nation in the back. However, it would also be the most complicated step in the process.

Before such a plebiscite could be held, a variety of procedural questions would have to be answered: how to define voter eligibility; where would balloting take place; what percentage, if any, of Palestinians would constitute a quorum; and how, given that many Palestinians live in nondemocratic societies, would it be possible to ensure free debate and prevent fraud and intimidation?

With regard to voter eligibility, the guiding principle should be comprehensiveness, with due regard for the difficulties posed by the physical dispersion of Palestinians. The population registers of the West Bank and Gaza and of UNRWA could provide a point of departure in identifying adult Palestinians, and these should be amended and supplemented by surveys, at least among the largest concentrations of Palestinians—i.e., those in the countries bordering Israel as well as in the Gulf region. For this purpose, it would be advisable to establish a special international commission, like those which have helped to oversee elections in the Philippines, Hungary, and Nicaragua. Such a commission could, in collaboration with the PLO, also define voting procedures and oversee the actual administration of the plebiscite. Needless to say, a plebiscite of this sort would be impossible without the cooperation of the relevant Arab states.

Even participatory ratification would not necessarily ensure the persistence of an environment supportive of peace. Over the long run, this would also depend on social and economic conditions in the area. Widespread unemployment, depressed living standards, inadequate delivery of public services, and intolerable inequalities would all create fertile ground for millenarian movements and demagogues who might well redirect passions stemming from domestic discontent against the peace settlement itself. Durable peace therefore also depends on a combination of deterrence and continuing socioeconomic well-being. However, beyond the signal of broad-based commitment to the settlement at the time it is contracted, popular ratification is necessary to deny rejectionists and revisionists a pretext for subsequently charging that the settlement did not represent the will of the people.

Conclusions

Like others before us, we have tried in this book to outline the basis for a resolution of the Israeli-Palestinian and Israeli-Arab conflicts. Unlike many others, we have together gone beyond generalities to describe or prescribe the substantive content of a settlement in a fairly comprehensive fashion. Still, we recognize that our conclusions are sometimes little more than guidelines, however elaborate, for the treatment of the major issues. In practice, many of these issues will have to be addressed in far greater detail. This is as true of the larger questions which we have probed (such as security arrangements, economic relations, and refugee resettlement) as it is of more marginal and/or technical matters which we have not even raised (e.g., extradition agreements and other legal affairs, assignment of radio and television frequencies, air traffic coordination, agreements on air and water pollution standards, etc.). Technical expertise would be needed during negotiations to deal both with the central issues, which should be resolved in all respects, and with the secondary questions, whose disposition should be specified in as much detail as possible. At the same time, given the limits of human foresight, it will be impossible to settle in advance every manifestation of such technical problems or to anticipate changing circumstances which might require different arrangements in the future. At a minimum, therefore, it will be necessary as part of a general settlement to establish flexible mechanisms, such as joint standing committees, to follow through on these matters and to adapt to the requirements of new economic or technological conditions.

In the larger scheme of things, however, such challenges are of secondary importance compared to the fundamental question of the political will to establish and maintain peace. To judge by the historical record, the most ardent proponents of a negotiated peace between Israel and the Arabs are neither Israelis nor Arabs. Instead, it is would-be mediators—foreign governments, voluntary organizations, and well-meaning individuals—who display the greatest impatience for a peace settlement. Between the two protagonists most directly involved, there has been an abstract desire for peace, but there has generally been far less enthusiasm for a negotiating process. There are four explanations for this attitude: some are deterred by the concessions that peace requires, some reject the very principle of negotiated peace, some are convinced that negotiations are futile, and some are convinced that real, durable peace is simply not possible.

The first attitude essentially involves bargaining terms. We believe that the substance of the two-state settlement described in this book provides the only viable basis for a settlement of the Israeli-Palestinian, hence the Israeli-Arab, conflict. There is, of course, no way to prove or disprove beyond a doubt the validity of this belief. Nevertheless, experience and reason strongly indicate that even the most determined effort by either side to pursue more ambitious objectives will produce, at best, continuing political stalemate, and at worst, greater damage to both sides.

The second position—opposition to a negotiated peace under any circumstances—generally prevailed on the Arab side until the late 1960s, when various Arab spokesmen began to speak of conditional acceptance rather than categorical rejection of peace with Israel. Although some fundamentalist and nationalist organizations still maintain a rejectionist posture, the situation has now evolved to the point where principled rejection of peace through compromise is not the declared policy of any major Arab government or of the PLO. For all practical purposes, this obstacle no longer exists, at least at the formal level. However, doubts remain on both sides about real intentions and hidden agendas. Among Palestinians, there are those who still believe that Israel is by internal design programmed to expand at the Arabs' expense and that Israeli statements about a willingness to negotiate are not credible. Consequently, there is no point even entering into negotiations.

In Israel, there are those who believe that Palestinian conciliatory statements are not to be trusted and that even if an agreement were achieved, it would not be honored, or, alternatively, that a two-state settlement is inherently unstable and would collapse regardless of the intentions of the other side. Given their skepticism about the possibility of a real, durable peace, these people also regard the negotiating process as a pointless exercise.

To some extent, these attitudes reflect a resigned fatalism that gives more weight to inscrutable forces of history than to human agency and that betrays introvertedness and cynicism as opposed to optimism. Such attitudes shut doors to creative policy making and become self-fulfilling prophecies of doom.

Moreover, the Israeli skepticism about the possibility of peace is also due in part to a tendency to equate peace with some idyllic vision of harmony in which there are no resentments, no animosities, no disputes, and no contradictions. This is a romantic view of history and politics that bears no relation to reality, even for countries like those in Western Europe, among whom the idea of war has become virtually unthinkable. Peace is not the absence of conflict, but rather a state of affairs in which conflicts that do exist are resolved or at least managed without the threat or use of force. Goodwill may encourage people and states to maintain this state of affairs over time, and goodwill may in turn be reinforced by the habit of peaceful coexistence, but the main factor in determining whether or not peace prevails is self-interest. The breakdown of peace and a reversion to active belligerency are not uncommon in history. Indeed, most wars have involved countries or peoples previously at peace. Nevertheless, launching a war or otherwise acting in ways that lead to war cannot be a frivolous decision, since some resistance must always be anticipated. Any leader choosing to renounce peace must therefore expect that his country will pay a price, but the price he is willing to pay will be directly related to the degree of dissatisfaction with the existing situation. The less tolerable the status quo, the higher the price he will accept to challenge it and the more damage that must be credibly threatened in order to deter him.

Conversely, a status quo which meets more needs or creates more vested interests in its perpetuation will make the leadership less motivated to run risks and incur costs in order to challenge it—i.e., it will raise the threshold for a decision in favor of war.

The type of settlement outlined in this book would not eliminate all grievances or satisfy all claims, but its overall parameters would meet many essential needs and create many constituencies whose interests would be jeopardized by a belligerent policy. It is therefore highly probable that rational Palestinian governments would not risk the loss of all that had been achieved in order to pursue even more ambitious objectives which would have very little chance of being realized. At least in the minimalist sense of the term, there is therefore no basis for assuming that peace is impossible.

On the other hand, of course, it is hardly a certainty. There can be no absolute assurance of perpetual peace because even the most stable, routine state of peace is no proof against irrationality, miscalculation, mass hysteria, unbridled ambitions, and irresponsible leadership. Furthermore, Israeli skepticism is fed not only by the expectation that frictions will persist or arise but also by the attribution of explicitly malevolent purposes to Palestinian interlocutors—i.e., by the conviction that the enmity of Palestinians and/or other Arabs toward Israel is implacable and that their conscious intention is not to abide by a peace agreement but simply to exploit it in order to improve their tactical position in some future war that is ultimately unavoidable. Such intentions cannot be conclusively proven, but they cannot be disproven either, and it is with such concerns in mind that security arrangements are incorporated into the agreement, attention is paid to the economic requirements of the various parties, and provisions are made for a comprehensive regional settlement and the active involvement of outside powers. Taken together, these measures provide a high degree of confidence that peace can and will be sustained.

It is true that peace of this sort, which at the bottom end of the scale can be described as institutionalized nonbelligerency, would meet basic political and security needs but would not provide the kind of emotional satisfaction or economic opportunity that would come from extensive interaction—often referred to as "normalization"—with the Arab world. Normalization, meaning the freedom to travel and do business throughout the Middle East at least on equal terms with other non-Arab, non-Moslem parties, is a powerful inducement. Indeed, it is envisaged as an integral part of the regional settlement. Nevertheless, it is not as evident that peace in this sense would emerge in the short term or endure over the long term. There is nothing that precludes this possibility, but sustained interaction would require clear mutual benefit and would be more vulnerable than mere nonbelligerency to interruptions for extraneous reasons; nonobservance or even abrogation of economic or cultural normalization agreements would be hard to deter because there would be less concern about retaliation in kind and a military response would be highly unlikely.

The same is true about the long-term status of essentially unilateral matters which are nevertheless of concern to the other side. One such matter is the character of the political system in the Palestinian state. The existence of liberal democracy in the Palestinian state would appear to be in Israel's interest, not because public opinion would necessarily be more disposed than would an authoritarian government to peaceful relations with Israel, but because democratic regimes generally tend less to whip up public hysteria and are in any event less capable of sudden and radical policy reorientations. Nevertheless, there is not much point trying to make a political settlement contingent on the creation of such a regime, because even if such a provision were incorporated into a peace agreement (and any written Palestinian constitution), there is little that Israel could do to enforce its continuing implementation or rectify any "violation"; the long-term prospects for Palestinian democracy would ultimately depend on Palestinian political culture and domestic economic and social conditions. (For some reflections on the possible structure of the Palestinian political system by one of the co-authors, see "Addendum: The Building Blocks of a Palestinian State.")

Demanding some treaty obligation to maintain a special connection, such as federal or confederal links, between a Palestinian state and Jordan would be similarly problematic. A particular intimacy between the West Bank and Jordan is in any event indicated by geographic proximity, family ties, and economic links. Moreover, Palestinians generally recognize the logic of special relations and the PLO has formally endorsed the principle of confederation. But the Israeli advantage which is anticipated from such a link—i.e., the moderating influence of the Jordanian government on Palestinian authorities presumably more inclined to disruptive behavior—will accrue regardless of the constitutional character of ties between the East and West Banks, so long as the Jordanian government is willing and able to exercise such influence. On the other hand, even a formal link enshrined in a peace treaty could not preclude the subsequent secession of the West Bank and/or Gaza from a union (though it might provide a legal casus belli). Nor would it provide any real assurance that the government in Amman would not—perhaps due to domestic reasons or pressure from other Arab states—tolerate or itself undertake the kinds of destabilizing actions which a Palestinian government is suspected, rightly or wrongly, of being likely to carry out.

In short, it is important to maintain a sense of proportion and an appreciation of both the limitations and the possibilities of a two-state settlement. Even if unrealistic expectations do not prevent a settlement, they will certainly produce widespread disillusionment thereafter and undermine what has been achieved. It should be obvious, for example, that no contractual agreement can immediately transform the Israeli-Palestinian or Israeli-Arab relationship from one of intense animosity to one of great affection and intimacy. Peace, at least in the early years, should therefore be viewed as a mechanism for damage limitation through coexistence rather than as the realization of a vision of brotherhood and goodwill.

On the other hand, excessive cynicism is also out of place. Even if an agreement is viewed primarily in instrumental terms, it may gradually contribute to more profound changes in the realm of perceptions and attitudes. Just the experience of coexistence in a different psychological and institutional context holds out the promise of significant attitudinal shifts in the future. The transitional arrangements, for example, are considered with precisely this potential in mind. Their immediate effect will be to permit the redirection of at least some material and human resources to more constructive purposes than the uncompromising pursuit of the conflict, but their more important purpose is to change states of mind. It may be utopian to expect Jews and Arabs to love each other—even the British and the French have not yet reached that stage—but it is not unreasonable to hope that the experience of a qualitatively different relationship will put an end to the negation and demonization of the past.

The Israeli-Arab conflict is not the only source of instability and hostility in the Middle East; the entire state system of the region is unsettled and there is a daunting range of social, economic, and communal problems which have never been adequately addressed. On the other hand, Israeli-Arab enmity is a major obstacle in its own right and a factor which complicates almost every other obstacle to human progress. A political settlement can change the emotional climate and clear a road which, if taken, may lead to deeper rapprochement and cooperation for the sake of security, prosperity, and the real peace denied the peoples of the Middle East for far too long.

Addendum: The Building Blocks of a Palestinian State

SARI NUSSEIBEH

A Palestinian state is not a theoretical project. It is already very much a partial reality. Objectively, this reality is manifest in the historical experience of self-administration by the Palestinians, especially in the occupied territories. Subjectively, it has especially become manifest through the experience of the intifada, highlighted by the Palestinian Declaration of Independence of November 1988. More than anything else, the intifada transformed the objective experience of self-administration into a consciously articulated national strategy for achieving independence: it is as if a history of vertical institution building had reached the point where further growth could only be achieved through spreading out horizontally, weaving the structure of self-government and self-determination.

In the West Bank, the Jordanian government in essence provided a horizontal "roof" for Palestinian self-administration through the years 1949–67. Palestinians practiced self-administration—i.e., administered their affairs as individuals—in all walks of life under the ultimate authority of the Jordanian Cabinet. Municipal affairs were conducted by locally elected municipal councils, government departments were manned by Palestinian personnel, and a network of institutionalized charity and voluntary organizations attended to those areas of population needs that could not be formally run by government departments. At this minimal level, a parallel situation existed in Gaza. However, due to the political "Jordanization" of the West Bank, Palestinians there also had access to further political rights within the Jordanian system, whether as members of Parliament or of the Cabinet itself. Thus, while the Palestinians did not practice national self-administration or self-determination, they nevertheless administered their own affairs within the context of the Jordanian political system. Jerusalem's political uniqueness was preserved through the special respect accorded by Palestinians as a whole to its Palestinian governor, whose authority (as distinct from that of the mayor) extended over a governorate which included Jericho in the East and reached almost to Nablus in the north and Hebron in the south.

Following the June 1967 war, this roof was partially replaced by the Israeli military authority. Palestinian personnel in the various Jordanian government departments (health, education, social welfare, etc.) simply came under the control of the Israeli military governor (later the head of the "civil administration"). Over the years, this administrative body underwent a natural process of growth, with the number of employees reaching approximately 25,000. Simultaneously, and because of the absence of an indigenous penultimate authority, the sector of voluntary associations and societies in public services also grew in response to the expanding needs of the population. Attention was concentrated on social welfare, preschool and post-high-school education, illiteracy, and health. However, the characteristic feature of this process of self-initiated and voluntary institution building was its "vertical" orientation. Nominally, all the registered societies which operated services ranging from universities to hospitals came under the single roof of a Federation of Charitable Societies. Actually, only a minimum degree of coordination existed. Professional unions were joined in a single federation, but this federation never envisaged, let alone implemented, a master development plan. A Higher Council of Education was established, but it was not empowered to institute an education-development master plan. At another level, a network of voluntary committees (e.g., health services) also mushroomed, but again the orientation was vertical rather than horizontal. This notwithstanding, therefore, it could be said that the self-administration component of a Palestinian state structure has been in existence for at least forty years, and the only basic element which was absent throughout these years has been a Palestinian roof, or government.

Soon after the intifada broke out in December 1987, the underground leadership of the uprising outlined its "battlefield" strategy as consisting of two complementary aims: to dismantle the Israeli network of administrative authority and to construct an alternative national authority, in preparation for a declaration of independence. Apart from anything else which it caused, or which it reflected, the intifada was also a revolution in mass consciousness, underlining the need for embodying the idea of self-determination in tangible structures in reality. The Jordanian decision in mid-

1988 to "disengage" legally and administratively from the West Bank acted as a further catalyst in this direction. Already, a wide-ranging grass-roots movement of popular committees was mushrooming throughout the occupied territories, reinforcing an already existing structure of voluntary work committees and institutions. The predominant orientation of this new construction, however, was still vertical. Even so, giant steps were taken in the process of state building. The Palestinian Declaration of Independence of November 1988 was regarded in one sense as an explicit national statement of intent: to work further toward establishing a government in Palestine and to conclude peace with Israel. The year 1990 witnessed a conscious national effort at weaving "horizontal structures." The Higher Council of Education was revitalized, higher councils in the labor and student sectors were established, a federation of women's committees was organized, and further efforts were being made in other sectors, including agriculture and industry. Within the PLO leadership, efforts were also being made to draw up a master economic development plan to make full use of international economic aid and to encourage the process of state building or "institutionalization" of the intifada. In this regard, it is not inconceivable that the stage will soon be reached when the PLO leadership, which has endorsed the principle of establishing a provisional government bureaucracy or structure, will indeed take the step of declaring the establishment of such a government. In so doing, it will simply be putting the already existing jigsaw pieces of bureaucracy together— the legal and religious institutions, the chambers of commerce and industry, the municipal and village councils, the civil administration work force, the clinics and hospitals, the schools and universities, the federations of societies and unions, the voluntary committees, and so forth. Indeed, when a government is finally established, it will find a fully equipped work force made up of both local Palestinians and returnees, from pilots to radio and television station technicians (many of whom are currently manning the bureaucracies of other Arab governments).

In terms of its political constitution, the Palestinian state will in all likelihood be fashioned in accordance with the main principles embodied in the Palestinian Declaration of Independence, endorsed by the Palestine National Council (PNC) in November 1988. The declaration states that "the state of Palestine is for Palestinians wherever they may be, in which they may be able to develop their national and cultural character, to enjoy complete equality in rights, to have their religious and political beliefs as well as their dignity protected, within the framework of a parliamentary democratic system which is based on the principles of freedom of expression, the freedom of party formation, the guarantee of the rights of the minority and the respect for the decisions of the majority, on social justice and equality, and on nondiscrimination in public rights on the basis of race, religion, or sex, and in accordance with a constitution that will guarantee the sovereignty of law and an independent judiciary system, and on the basis of a total recognition of Palestine's spiritual and cultural heritage, and the principle of tolerance and coexistence among religions."

In accordance with these principles, one assumes that the government of Palestine will establish, as in other democracies, a constitutional model that will ensure the independence from the executive of the judicial and

legislative branches of government. One of the primary
tasks of the legislative branch would have to be to weave
the principles of the Palestinian Declaration of Independence into a constitution that will once and for all
repeal the British Mandatory Emergency Laws (which
have been a nightmare for Palestinians ever since their
enactment in 1945) and guarantee the rights of individuals, including the basic right of free expression. The
constitution should also guarantee public rights, and
perhaps a special provision could be incorporated which
would require the holding of a referendum on such
major national issues as the decision to become confed-
erated with other states. As for the judicial system, it
would be well if, among other provisions, the practice
of "trial by jury" is enacted as law. This would serve
several purposes at once. It would ensure that the legal
system is not the province solely of an "expert sector"
of society, it would encourage a formalized extension
of existing traditional practices of community involvement in the adjudication of conflicts and disagreements,
it would serve as a useful educational mechanism for
involvement in communal and democratic decision-
making processes, and it would encourage the development of a sense of responsibility toward the state.
Otherwise, the system of civil law which is already in
existence and which has its twin part in the kingdom of
Jordan can be applied.

Concerning the executive branch of government, and
drawing on the experience of other democracies, it
would be advisable if there were to be direct national
presidential elections, held every five or six years. These
elections will ensure for the chief executive of the state
the tipping balance in political decisions which have a
national character. On the other hand, bearing in mind

the regional affinities of the population, it would be advisable to divide the state into five electoral departments, a northern department centered in Nablus, a central department in East Jerusalem, a southern department in Hebron, and departments in Gaza and in Khan Yunis or Rafah. Elections for parliamentary representatives can then be held on a regional basis, perhaps once every four years, with each department sending a number of representatives proportional to the size of its population to the House of Representatives. While parties may form coalitions, it would be the individuals themselves who would be elected in their respective departments and who would be directly answerable to their constituents. Governments can then be formed by any party or coalition of parties that has a majority of representatives. Bylaws can be enacted to define the powers of the President and the Cabinet. The aim should be to strike a balance between these two branches of the executive, ensuring a predominant weight in the decision-making process for the Cabinet in regional matters (e.g., budgets for development plans) and for the President in national matters (e.g., external relations). The system of referendums can ensure that ultimate direct sovereignty rests with the people themselves. Thus, the system would benefit from the most positive combination of the various types of Western democracies.

It is natural to assume that parties which will be formed in the Palestinian state will be historically affiliated with those factions within the PLO structure that will wish to participate in the process of state building. However, it is also natural to assume that party platforms must conform to the general principles and foundation agreements on which the state is based. Therefore, each party's competitive distinctiveness must have to do with its economic and social vision for construction rather than with irredentist ideological rhetoric. In this context, the regionalization of elections will go a long way toward ensuring that the system will address tangible development needs. Both the representatives themselves and the central functions of the representative government will be directed toward the fulfillment of the regional needs of the electorate.

The main immediate task for the Palestinian government should be construction, rehabilitation, and economic development. Twenty-eight refugee camps spread throughout the West Bank and Gaza should be replaced by townships and extended suburbs. Urban construction should also be addressed to the expanding housing needs of the existing population as well as Palestinian returnees. Planning for the latter should be based on a conservative estimate of 1.5 million individuals. Obviously, the implementation of an urban rehabilitation program will have to take place in stages, and the absorption of returnees will have to be worked out over a period of time, perhaps three to five years. Urban rehabilitation will involve housing as well as associated infrastructure. In Gaza, the density of the population and the limited size of the area would make the construction of high-rise apartments the preferable course, whereas in the West Bank several options would be available, including the establishment of new townships, especially in the outlying areas. These new townships will require major infrastructure work, including roads, water systems, electricity, telecommunications, etc. Palestinian development planning experts estimate that infrastructural expansion in existing residential areas can accommodate the absorption of approximately 750,000 individuals, while it is possible to establish at least three new towns in areas which are already agriculturally developed (in the northern Jordan Valley, the Jenin and Hebron areas) which would absorb a further 200,000 individuals. A positive by-product of this expansion, including the possible construction of residential facilities in outlying areas, would be to make unutilized land more accessible and therefore more easily available for reclamation. Local Palestinian agricultural engineers estimate that, if the land confiscation measures over the past twenty-three years are rendered null and void, it is possible to double the area that can be agriculturally utilized. This expansion of the cultivated area notwithstanding, experts estimate that sufficient land would still be available for a major urban development program. However, strict measures should be taken to ensure that such development does not harm the environment. Needless to say, the work on construction (urban and infrastructural) and on land reclamation (during and after) would create thousands of new jobs (at both the labor and professional/technician levels). A redesign of the road transportation system (to account for major highway corridors, especially linking northern and southern areas) would involve the construction of approximately 2,900 kilometers, an increase of 41 percent over the existing system. This would include, according to local engineering and planning experts, a major highway running into Gaza from northern Sinai, which could then cross Israeli territory as far as Idnah in the West Bank, continue along a ring road around Jerusalem, and head eastward into Jordan. A transitional expressway such as this would facilitate economic linkages among Egypt, Israel, Palestine, and Jordan, and all these countries can jointly invest in its construction.

In addition to having to concentrate on the immediate urban-development needs and rehabilitation, the Palestinian government should also define as another priority target the establishment of a "welfare" structure, as well as a social rehabilitation program: health and national insurance schemes, labor-protection laws and retirement benefits, educational opportunities, and so forth. From historical experience, it would seem advisable that the state not interfere with the economy except to the extent that it ensures an acceptable minimum level of welfare for its citizens. Bearing in mind the expected psychological upheaval associated with major demographic and political changes, the government must also devote special attention to social-welfare and social-guidance work and to child welfare. At all events, a top priority for the state leadership will be to attend to the needs and requirements of a historically underprivileged and deprived community, especially the refugee population both inside and outside the area. Among other things, this will also mean having to develop the appropriate educational rehabilitation and technical training system to synchronize work-force supply and demand in the manner that is most conducive to economic growth and the national interest.

Economically speaking, the Palestinian state's main resource will be its human reservoir of skilled laborers and technicians, its professionals and its educated population. While existing economic figures and statistics do not reflect accurately what the picture will look like once the state is established and major demographic changes begin to take place, yet such figures may be helpful, and they may in some areas be typical. Of a total population of approximately 1.6 million individuals in the West Bank (including East Jerusalem) and Gaza, nearly 50 percent are under fourteen years of age, portending a major productive potential. The school population alone stands at nearly 500,000. Almost 300,000 Palestinians are registered employees (more than half of whom are laborers, of which more than half again are employed in or by Israel, mostly in construction). These figures include employees in other sectors, as well as almost 42,000 who are registered as agricultural employees. However, nearly 80,000 Palestinians are working in the agricultural sector, many of whom are farmers, and nearly 50 percent of whom in the West Bank are small farmers who have less than twenty dunams. The agricultural sector accounts for nearly 35 percent of the gross national product, while the industrial sector (primarily because of restrictions) has not grown beyond the 7 percent of GNP which it contributed before 1967. According to a recent study by economic experts, it is estimated that in the context of a peace scenario, the growth rate of the gross national product of the West Bank/Gaza region (which has declined since 1979) will reach the 6 percent level. However, this estimate is based on population calculations that do not take into account returnees or realistic development plans, including plans to develop the industrial sector, which these economic experts admit has "lagged behind." Generally speaking, however, these experts estimate that in the context of a peace scenario, investment will increase by as much as 50 to 100 percent in the various countries in the region. Thus, even in the context of a peace scenario that does not account for the establishment of an independent Palestinian state, or even an Israeli withdrawal (if such a scenario is at all realistic in the first place), these experts estimate that the GNP in the West Bank/Gaza region could have reached as much as $2,650 million (from an estimated $1,480 million in 1982) if investments had increased from $315 million in 1982 to $650 million in 1992.

Palestinian economic experts, on the other hand, have even brighter predictions. Hypothesizing the existence of a state, George Abed in a recently published paper, "The Economic Viability of a Palestinian State," estimates a GNP of $3,500 million (in 1990 prices), accounting for the repatriation of approximately 750,000 returnees and external aid for their rehabilitation. Abed also points out that the share of industry in the gross national product should increase from its present level of 7 percent to what he calls "a more normal" 30 to 35 percent (a variable which is absent in the previously cited economic study). Speaking generally, the economy can be developed in the industrial (e.g., science and technology, cottage industries, etc.) as well as in the services sectors (e.g., tourism and financial services). According to Abed's calculations, a comprehensive development plan (encompassing the construction of the required physical and social infrastructure) will cost about $13 billion (in 1990 prices). If one also includes the investments needed to raise productivity in the industrial, agricultural, agro-industrial, and services sectors, a grand total of $23 billion will be required over an extended period (e.g., ten years), of which the share of the public sector in the same period could reach $12 billion, mostly generated from the services of the infrastructural facilities themselves.

The Abed study also addresses the structural question of how the Palestinian state's economy will be designed.

In his view, and taking into account the experience of the Palestinians themselves as well as the developments in the socialist world at large, it is reasonable to expect that Palestinians will favor an economic system "that allows a dominant role for the private sector, where the price mechanism is the primary instrument for the allocation of resources, where fiscal and regulatory policies are designed to ensure adequate incentives while mitigating the maldistribution of income and wealth, and where the exchange and trade system is virtually free of controls." However, one must not ignore economic policies and ideas that may be derived from indigenous Islamic principles, especially those that address the welfare and taxation systems. In any case, the essential balance to achieve in any successful system is that which minimizes state control while ensuring a reasonable growth rate, efficiency, and an acceptable level of welfare and living standards. One way to bypass state bureaucracy while preserving control may be through a system of independent public authorities which are organized within the law but fall outside the direct influence of the state apparatus. These can be utilized for the provision of certain facilities (e.g., electricity, telecommunications, transportation, etc.).

An independent Palestinian state, however, should not and cannot be an isolated entity in the region. To be an independent state does not mean to be an economically self-sufficient state, or a hermetically sealed state, and indeed many if not most existing states are not economically self-sufficient, nor can they be socially or culturally self-sustaining. On the contrary, Palestine should seek to integrate itself with neighboring countries, joining with them in the regional venture to make the best use of existing resources and economic potentials. The very existence of Palestine should serve as a stabilizing factor in the region, facilitating economic growth and prosperity. The fact that Palestinians who are currently dispersed in the Arab world, dispossessed, disenfranchised, and desperate, can finally converge together in a country that they know to be their own, where they can enjoy the political rights due to a human being, and where they can exert themselves constructively in building together a common future for themselves—all this will defuse political tension in the Arab world, whether by Palestinians themselves or purportedly on their behalf. Economic prosperity, both in Palestine and in the region as a whole, will further reduce tensions. But if Palestine is to be a catalyst for peace and prosperity in the region, it must first be free. Once independent and free, Palestine can then work to be a partner to all those nations and states that strive to create a better and safer world.

Index

Abbas, Abul, 17, 49
Abed, George, 170
Abu Dis (West Bank), 116
agriculture, 167; irrigation, 110; labor, 169; outlook for, 167, 170
air defense, Israeli, 64, 69
al-Fajr, 47
Allon Plan, 100
Alon Shvut (West Bank), 99
al-Ram (West Bank), 116
Amirav, Moshe, 48–49, 119–20
Anata (West Bank), 116
aquifers, 31, 108–9, 110; agreements on, 84, 108, 110
Arab Higher Committee (1940s), 35
Arab-Israeli conflict, 21, 53–54, 125–27, 149–51, 153, 156–57; economic embargo against Israel, 131; potential future threat, 63, 65, 66–67, 69, 74; refugee problem as essence of, 86, 129; regional approach to solutions, 9, 125–34; re-Palestinization of, 14, 53–57, 133; risk minimization, 72, 132; role of water resources in, 107, 113, 125, 128–29; War of 1967, 6, 21, 76, 107
Arab League, 130
Arab meetings: 182 (Fez peace plan), 38, 127; 1990 Baghdad

summit, 128; *see also* Palestine National Council
Arabs: in Israel, 13, 104, 105; 1948 invasion of Israel by, 54; and Palestinian Arabs, 13–14, 53, 55, 125
Arab world, 9, 125–29, 133–34; attitudes toward two-state solution, 57–59, 126–29, 151; financial aid obligation to Palestine, 130; and Gulf crisis, 14, 21, 55; Palestinian peace proposal endorsed by, 127–29; Palestinian refugee camps in, 86, 87–88, 129; Palestinians in, 87–90, 129; PLO not speaking for, 87–90, 129
Arafat, Yasir, 18, 20, 49
Ariel (West Bank), 101–2, 104
Armistice of 1949, 134; border line of, 76, 78, 115, 117; *see also* Green Line
arms control agreements, 66, 70, 71, 125, 132
arms race, Middle East, 125
army, Israeli, 63, 68
artesian wells, 109
Assad, Hafez al-, 46
asymmetry, situational, 30–31, 58, 62
Atarot (Jerusalem), 116